Teenagers Are People Too!

by
Joyce Meyer

To: Britni
Christmas 2003

From: Mom

Warner Faith

WARNER BOOKS

An AOL Time Warner Company

Unless otherwise indicated, all Scripture quotations are taken from *The Amplified Bible* (AMP). *The Amplified Bible, Old Testament*, copyright © 1965, 1987 by The Zondervan Corporation. *The Amplified New Testament*, copyright © 1954, 1958, 1987 by The Lockman Foundation. Used by permission.

Scripture quotations marked "NASB" are taken from the *New American Standard Bible®*, (NASB®), Copyright © The Lockman Foundation 1960, 1962, 1963, 1968, 1971, 1972, 1973, 1975, 1977. Used by permission.

Scripture quotations marked "NIV" are taken from the *Holy Bible, New International Version®*. NIV®. Copyright © 1973, 1978, 1984 by International Bible Society. used by permission of Zondervan Publishing House. All rights reserved.

Scripture quotations marked "NKJV" are taken from the *New King James Version*. Copyright © 1982, by Thomas Nelson, Inc. Used by permission. All rights reserved.

Scripture quotations marked "KJV" are taken from the *King James Version* of the Bible.

Scripture quotation marks "TEV" are from the *Today's English Version—Second Edition* © 1992 by American Bible Society. Used by permission.

WARNER BOOKS EDITION

Copyright © 2002 by Joyce Meyer
Life In The Word, Inc.
P.O. Box 655
Fenton, Missouri 63026
All rights reserved.

Warner Books, Inc., 1271 Avenue of the Americas, New York, NY 10020

Visit our Website at www.twbookmark.com.

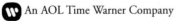 An AOL Time Warner Company

Printed in the United States of America
First Warner Faith Printing: October 2002
10 9 8 7 6 5 4 3 2 1

ISBN: 0-446-69112-7
LCCN: 2002110915

Dedication

I wish to dedicate this book to my son Daniel. God spoke to his father and me in our hearts to have him at a time in our life when we thought we were finished having children. Once again God surprised us.

Daniel has been a tremendous blessing to us. He has always been full of zest for life, had an abundance of energy and loved to have fun. He is caring; he loves to take care of people, especially those who are hurting or in need. We have always recognized in him a compassionate heart and a sensitivity to help people and have always felt that God gave him to us for a great purpose in His kingdom.

Around the age of fourteen Daniel began to talk to us about his desire to work with youth someday. Many young people change their mind monthly about what they want to do in life, but Dan always stuck to his original vision. He did other things in the ministry as he grew up.

He worked in the warehouse, traveled with us working behind the tape table, set up television equipment, served as a cameraman and was one of our top television editors. But he was always open with us about the fact that someday he knew he would work with youth.

Dan, you have already made your dad and me very proud of you, but I believe the marvelous things you will do with your life are only beginning. You are on the very threshold of great and mighty exploits. God has blessed you with a wonderful wife in Charity, and I know that as the two of you step out to follow your dreams, we will not be disappointed in you.

We are very happy to be in ministry with you reaching out to the youth of our generation. I believe with us working together, and with the help of the awesome team of people God has given us, we have an opportunity to make a difference in this world and to help an unlimited number of young people find a deep personal relationship with Jesus Christ, as well as fulfill His call on their lives.

Contents

Foreword

Adults look at the next generation and can't understand why kids are killing kids, why teen pregnancy and suicide rates keep rising, why their kids are more interested in going to a keg party than church. They can't understand why teenagers are doing things "they would never have dreamed of doing when they were that age."

We cannot live in a society that was built on the foundation of God's Word and, once the building is finished, try to remove that foundation. A moral catastrophe is inevitable.

As our culture moves further away from the biblical truths from which our moral fabric was woven, teenagers find it harder and harder to follow rules and guidelines which seem archaic and impractical in today's world. But where does society's influence end and personal responsibility begin?

Let's make a decision to breed respect by showing respect.

Parents, you cannot expect your children to be responsible to obey you if you never release any authority to them. Teenagers, if you want your parents to be patient with you, start sowing seeds by being patient with them. Realize that some of the changes in every generation are always hard on those who are still around from the previous generation.

If you're wondering what Joyce Meyer, successful mother of four, knows about teenagers, just read the advice above. It's hers. And it's just a taste of the perspective-shifting wisdom this book has to offer. (Was it mentioned that she's a successful mother of four?) She speaks from years of experience, not just theory.

Never have teenagers had such comprehensive blueprints into the world of adulthood. There are some adults who have spent years searching for these guidelines on spiritual and emotional maturity. Using the Bible as God's ultimate prescription on how to live a successful, outrageously wonderful life, Joyce Meyer tackles the most relevant issues teenagers face: emotional pain and disappointment, fear, loneliness, overcoming your past, priorities in relationships and the future.

You have tremendous worth and value. You had the vulnerability to pick up this book and ask for guidance. And you have the courage to start making the decisions now which will affect your future and make a difference in the world around you. By incorporating these valuable lessons, you are not only making a difference in *your* generation, but also the *next*.

The decisions you make today are the building blocks for your future. Make them wisely.

Consumed by the Call,

— Ron Luce

President of Teen Mania Ministries

Preface

I have heard an abundance of talk concerning the fact that teenagers need to show more respect for adults, and, of course, that is true. It is also true that adults need to show more respect not only to teenagers, but to children in general.

Sometimes as adults we act as though children are not really people, at least not important people like we think we are. This type of an attitude is offensive to God Who created all of us — including teenagers — and respects each of us.

The Lord has been dealing with me personally about taking more time to talk with young people, not judging them according to their outward appearance, but realizing that many of them have strong gifts, including gifts of leadership, and letting them be themselves.

Most of the management of one organization I deal with are all under thirty years of age. As I met with all of them several months ago, it began to sink into my middle-aged brain that I might be missing some opportunities by not hiring more people directly out of high school or college. Businesses usually want "experienced help"; however, nobody ever gets any experience unless given a chance. Someone gave me a job when I was still in school, and I can do the same thing for others.

The last thing I ever thought I would be doing is writing a book for teenagers; however, as we all know, God likes to surprise us.

Several years ago God placed a burden upon my heart for the young people of our generation. I began to pray for Him to raise up leaders who would be good examples for them — heroes they could admire, whose example they could follow. I prayed for these leaders to be people of character who would display honesty, truthfulness, respect for everyone, excellence, integrity, honor, faithfulness, a willingness to sacrifice, faith against all odds and hope in seemingly hopeless circumstances — young men and women of courage and boldness who would be willing to step out on the front lines and make a difference in their generation.

In our society today, we need young people with the spirit of Joshua, a young man with a courageous spirit who refused to be satisfied with the status quo. When others believed they could do nothing, Joshua believed he could do whatever God told him to do. When others were negative, he was positive — a necessary trait in anyone who intends to succeed in life.[1]

I would like to say that I love young people. I pray that my ministry will be a great blessing to multiplied millions of them and that it will inspire them to be all they can be for God and His glory.

I believe in young people. They are talented, creative, courageous, awesome, refreshing and vital to the future of any nation. With great admiration and respect I have written this book, and I pray that I have chosen to cover the subjects that are the most needed for the youth of today.

Introduction:
Teenagers Are People Too!

As a teenager reading this book, you may look at my picture in the back and think, *What can a woman her age know about being a teenager?*

Well, believe it or not, I once was your age, and, believe it or not, someday you will be as old as I am now. The decisions you make between now and then will determine the quality of life you have. Every decision you make right now is affecting your future — the attitude you have toward family, school and church; the kind of friends and the type of entertainment you choose; the role models you follow and the heroes you admire and imitate — all these have lasting results. They are not fleeting things without impact on the rest of your life.

As a young person, it may be harder for you to make proper decisions than it is for an adult, but that is understandable.

Teenagers are no different from anyone else. They have many of the same problems adults have, but they are less equipped to deal with them simply due to lack of experience.

At age eighteen, we usually think we know everything, and certainly more than our parents and most adults we know. By age forty, we have realized we don't know much of anything and need all the wisdom we can get. At this point in life, we usually begin to gain some wisdom, much of which derives from the experiences we have had.

The fact is, we learn much more about life from the things we go through than we ever do from books.

<u>We gain knowledge from books; we gain experience from life</u>.

Some teens do have more common sense than adults. Not all adults are doing what they should be doing in life. It seems almost everyone has personal problems, and I have observed that people with problems usually cause problems for those they are in relationship with.

You as a teenager may be facing some difficult problems in your life right now. Those problems did not just appear suddenly; there is a reason, a root cause for them. But there is also a solution.

In this book, we are going to explore some of those problems, their causes and ways to overcome them. In the process, you will discover that regardless of your past, God has a wonderful future planned for you.

Face Challenges Together

Your teen years can be challenging not only for you, but for your parents as well. You may be living with both of your parents or in a single-parent household, you may be living with a relative or a legal guardian, or it is possible you are reading this book and currently have no place you call home. Whatever your present situation, because it is very probable that you will face some kind of challenges as a teenager, I have included a special section for parents at the end of this book.

In this final chapter they will read about some of the pressures teens are under these days that can cause you to make unwise decisions about your behavior, and they will be encouraged to be patient, loving, respectful and supportive of you. The ultimate purpose is to help close the "generation gap" and encourage each of you that you *can* live together in peace, harmony and love.

I believe that God wants your teen years to be a happy, healthy, exciting time of life, one filled with positive learning experiences. I pray that reading this book will be one of those positive experiences for you in which you will learn that God loves you, your parents love you, and with God's help, you can overcome every problem and become the person He created you to be!

one

Unconditional Love and Acceptance

I t seems to me that things would be so much better if we could all be referred to just as "people," not so much as "children," "teenagers," "young adults," "the elderly," "middle-aged," "men" or "women," "short" or "tall," "skinny" or "fat," "white," "black," "brown," "red" or "yellow." We continually classify one another, and somehow in doing so, I think we automatically exclude many people who are not seen to be in our classification. If not as drastic as exclusion, then certainly we usually place an uncomfortable distance between us.

> *Even as [in His love] He chose us [actually picked us out for Himself as His own] in Christ before the foundation of the world. . . .*
> *Ephesians 1:4*

We admit that we need others who are different from us, but somehow when faced with them we tend either to reject or try to change them. Instead of thinking that different is bad, we must understand once and for all that <u>different is good</u>.

All we have to do is look at each other to see that God is certainly fond of variety. We all have different fingerprints and DNA, a variety of blood types, voices, body shapes and sizes, color and texture of hair. We look different, and we have a wide variety of gifts and talents. If God had intended for us to be clones of one another, surely He would have arranged for all of us to be just alike.

Often teenagers are rejected by adults because they are different. They have different ideas, different hair and clothing styles, etc. With all of my heart I want to see people accept themselves, know they are accepted by God and begin to press forward to fulfill their God-ordained destiny.

No Strings Attached

Every human being on the earth seeks unconditional love and acceptance. It is the number one basic need of all people.

Teenagers are people too!]

<u>A teenager has the same needs as anyone else</u>. Each of us is created with the need to be loved and accepted, and God intends for us to experience that love and acceptance. He gives it to us willingly and abundantly. The problem is that we are so accustomed to not getting it from people, that by the time most of us enter into a personal relationship with God, we cannot believe He would give it to us either. (If you do not have a personal relationship with the Lord and you would like to, there is a prayer you can pray later on in this chapter.)

God is holding out to us the free gift of His unconditional love and acceptance, and we don't know how to receive it. What a tragedy! Free gifts are to be received and appreciated. You can receive from Jesus what others may not be giving you — a sense of value and worth, unconditional love and total acceptance as a person.

God already knows we don't deserve His goodness according to our merits, but He has blessed us and given us the opportunity to be in relationship with Jesus Christ, His Son, our Savior, Lord, Brother and Friend.[1]

A Brand-New Start

Having a personal relationship with Jesus cannot be equated with church attendance. Those who love the Lord will want to go to a good church and have fellowship with like-minded people. They will want to learn and worship Him with others. But before church can be truly enjoyed, an individual must first have a personal relationship with God through His Son Jesus Christ.

Jesus said . . . , I am the Way and the Truth and the Life; no one comes to the Father except by (through) Me (John 14:6). No amount of our own good works will gain us favor with God or ensure us a place in His eternal kingdom. Only faith in Jesus will do that — faith in Jesus is the key.

Perhaps your parents were believers who tried to instill faith in you as a child. Perhaps they took you to church and saw that you were exposed to the teaching of God's Word. You may have tried to follow the rules you were taught, but it all seemed so boring, and none of the people there seemed very happy. It may be that even your parents did not live the life at home they were telling you to live. They may have seemed hypocritical to you.

There is a major difference in having religion and having a personal relationship with God through Jesus Christ. Joining a church does not make one a Christian; faith in God through Jesus does.

You don't have to shut God out of your life because some church did not meet your needs. Like everything else in life, there are good churches and there are bad churches. You may be sick and go to a bad doctor, but you don't stop going to doctors just because of one bad experience. You keep looking until you find one who can help you with your sickness. The same is true of looking for the right church. Even a church can disappoint you, but God won't if you trust Him.

Your parents and others you looked up to may have been model Christians. They may have done every-thing right, and yet you could never seem to "hook into" what they said they believed. It just did not seem to be for you. You wished it would work for you; you wanted to feel close to God, but something was missing.

We went through this with our older son David when he was a teenager. There was continual strife between us. He went to church but lived a compromising life. We wanted him to be serious with God and make right choices, but he was consistently rebellious.

God showed me that I had unforgiveness toward him because he was not what I wanted him to be spiritually. I realized that I needed to accept him where he was and trust God to get him where he needed to be.

David felt rejected by his father and me. Although we loved him, we were rejecting him as he was. We wanted him to change, and he felt the pressure of our disapproval.

I knew that I needed to apologize to him and try to find a place of "new beginnings" in our relationship. His dad and I talked with him and told him if he would go to church once a week, not listen to heavy metal rock music in the house and not bring girls there while we were gone, we would not nag him about other things. We told him we recognized that he was eighteen years old and that it was time to let him make his own decisions.

From my experience with David I learned that a parent cannot make a child love God. That is something that must be worked out between God and every individual personally. But a parent can continue to pray for that child, love that child unconditionally and trust God with their outcome.

As we talked together, David began to cry. He told us that with all of his heart he wished he felt the way we did about God, but that something was missing for him, and he could not make himself have it. He said he needed our unconditional love and acceptance. He admitted that he was not living the way he should, but he felt he needed some time to make his own decisions without pressure from us.

The next few months were not easy for me. It was hard not to tell David what he should be doing. It was also hard to treat him right when he ignored what he knew were our wishes. There were a few occasions when things got a little tense, but for the most part we stuck to our agreement.

Six months passed. One evening David returned from a New Year's Eve church service and stated that God had dealt with him. He announced that he was going to go to Bible college in Florida. He said he intended to serve God if it was the last thing he ever did. I remember him standing in the living room and telling us that even if it meant he would lose all of his friends, he was going to follow God.

To make a rather long story short, David is now the Director of World Missions at our ministry, Life In The Word. He is married to a wonderful woman, has two lovely children and is a great joy to Dave and me.

We took David to church all of his life, but that was not enough to make him want to love and serve the Lord. Church attendance alone is not the answer — only a new birth can truly change a person's heart.

In John 3:3, Jesus said that in order to see the kingdom of God, a person must be born again. Without Jesus living in our heart we are spiritually dead. As we receive Him by faith into our heart to dwell there and ask Him to forgive our sins, we are cleansed, forgiven and made a new creature in Him.[2] At the new birth, we are given a brand-new start in life.

Do you need a brand-new start? If so, it is available to you by simply committing your life to Jesus Christ and asking Him to be Savior and Lord of your life. He gives us a reason to live, direction and purpose.

"Don't Worry — I'll Catch You"

Usually the plan of salvation is presented in the back of most Christian books; however, I am plainly laying out the plan early in the book. I don't want anyone to have to read this entire book and not know the joy of experiencing the unconditional love and acceptance of Jesus living in their heart.

The plan is simple. All you have to do is realize that you cannot live a good and holy life without God's help. You make mistakes; you are a sinner (as we all are); and you need forgiveness and help.

God has created us to need Him. If we are created to need Him, then we can never do anything but need Him, and we will never be fulfilled and satisfied without Him. Every one of us has a God-shaped hole inside us that only He can fill. We usually spend our lives trying to fill it with everything else — with friends, success, drugs, alcohol, cars, clothes, sex, possessions and accomplishments in life — but none of these will satisfy us or fill the empty void we have inside.

God wants to help us with life. He wants to make the hard things easy and the impossible things possible. All that is required of us is a complete surrender of our heart and life to His leadership. It is an act done by faith.

In Romans 10:9,10 we are told:

... if you acknowledge and confess with your lips that Jesus is Lord and in your heart believe (adhere to, trust in, and rely on the truth) that God raised Him from the dead, you will be saved.

For with the heart a person believes (adheres to, trusts in, and relies on Christ) and so is justified (declared righteous, acceptable to

God), and with the mouth he confesses (declares openly and speaks out freely his faith) and confirms [his] salvation.

In our society today, we tend to think that we must understand everything with our mind, but some things can only be understood with the heart. Most of us don't understand electricity, but we use it every day to bring light and power into our homes. In the same way, none of us can ever fully understand the plan of salvation with our mind. Salvation is not something we grasp intellectually; it is something we receive spiritually by faith. Don't try to understand God; simply believe.

In the Bible we read that Jesus came to earth as the Son of God; He was born of a virgin. Mary was His mother in the flesh, and God was His Father by the Holy Spirit — a miracle.[3] Remember, miracles cannot be explained.

God sent His only Son to die for us on a cross and to pay the price for our sins. The Lord loved us so much that He wanted to redeem us from the terrible condition into which we had fallen. To do that, He was ready to pay any price, and He did pay a high price indeed — the suffering and bloodshed of His Son to pay for the sins of many sons and daughters who would be eternally lost to Him without this sacrifice.[4]

Jesus took the punishment that we deserved. He suffered in your place and mine. He died and was buried, but on the third day He was resurrected from the dead and is alive today.[5] Jesus died for you!

God has done everything for us. All He asks us to do is believe. Simple childlike faith is all that is required.

It is like a young child jumping off a porch rail into his father's waiting arms, not fearful of getting hurt because Daddy has said, "Don't worry, I'll catch you." That is what God tells you and me when we put our trust in Him.[6]

If you have an earthly father you cannot trust, it may be harder for you to trust God, but you don't have to be afraid to trust Him. Surrender is the beginning of trust. As you will see next, surrendering your life to the Lord is not a negative thing; it is one of the best decisions you will ever make. It sets you free to enjoy the wonderful life God has planned for you.

God Will Take Care of You

I admit that complete surrender is a tall order. Abandonment of our life to another when we have no experience with that person is frightening to most of us.

The only thing I can assure you of is this:

God is good.

Every plan He has for you is good.

He may not always lead you in the way you would choose to go, but He will lead you the best way.

He will take care of you. What you commit to His trust, He will protect.

God will not always tell you ahead of time what He is going to do in your life. As I mentioned before, He likes surprises. Also, this is His method of teaching us to trust Him.

God does not give us all the answers because trust requires some unanswered questions. He will not allow any one of us to have everything all figured out.

If you have not yet surrendered your life to Jesus Christ, I want to encourage you to stop right now and do so. You can ask a Christian friend to pray with you or you can pray by yourself. Just be honest with God. He is your Father. Talk to Him as a dear Friend. You can tell Him anything and everything. He will never reject you nor judge you critically.

Start Your New Life

Here is a sample prayer you can use as a guideline:

Dear Father, I love You very much. I don't know You very well, but I believe that You know me. I believe in Your Son Jesus. I believe He died for me, shed His blood for me and paid for my sins. He took the punishment I deserved. I am so grateful that You and He have done this for me that I want to serve You all the rest of my life.

I know that I am a sinner. I admit my sins and confess them. I want to turn away from them and live a good clean life.

Lord Jesus, I surrender to You completely. I invite You to come and live in my heart, to lead and guide me all the rest of my days. I want to be born again, to know that my name is written in the Book of Life and that I will go to heaven when I die. I also want to have the assurance that You will be with me always and that, according to Your promise in the Bible, You will never leave me nor forsake me.[7]

Lord, by faith, I believe I am saved, that I am a new creature in Christ. You have forgiven all my sins and have given me a brand-new start.

Thank You, Father, for sending Jesus to die for me. In Jesus' name, amen.

If you sincerely prayed that prayer, you are now born again. You are part of God's family. I encourage you to call any of the numbers listed in the back of this book or write to the address given, and we will help you in any way we can. Just let us know that you accepted Christ as you were reading this book, and we will assist you in getting your new life as a Christian started right.

God's Mercy

When we deal with ordinary people, they usually are not very merciful. It seems we get into trouble each time we make a mistake. If we don't do exactly as they expect us to, they become angry, reject us and even punish us if they can.

God is just the opposite. It is His nature to be merciful. He enjoys giving people mercy, being good to those who least deserve it and giving people a second chance in life.

I don't think there are many things in life that hurt us emotionally as much as rejection. We all greatly desire acceptance. In order for people to accept us, they must know how to flow in mercy. Sad to say, very few people know how to do this.

The Bible tells us that God's mercy is new every day. (Lamentations 3:22,23.) That is really good news. I imagine you are like me and everyone else; you need mercy every day. We all make mistakes daily. People frequently reject us for our mistakes, but God does not. He helps us overcome them and improve. He teaches and trains us to do better because He loves us so much, but there is no pressure to be perfect.

You must believe by faith that God loves and accepts you and that He will never reject you as long as you believe in Him. (John 3:18.) This is the only way to enjoy unconditional love in the world we live in; we must receive it from God.

Too often we look to people to give us what only God can give. I did this for many years of my life, and it always ended in heartache. I was always disappointed with people.

People all have inherent (built-in) weaknesses; therefore, they can never be perfect.

We are all flawed; that is why we must have God's help continually in our lives. When we expect people to give us what only God can give us, we are doomed to disappointment. God wants us to look to Him, not to others. When we don't, He shows us the weakness in the people we are overly dependent upon. And He does it for our ultimate good.

There are times in life when God allows us to be hurt in order to help us. He is not the author of these times, but He will make them work to our advantage. Part of our personal and spiritual growth takes place in these times. God uses the hurts from our past to make us a better person in the future. It is the same principle that a good parent uses with a child they love.

I did not spank or correct my children because I enjoyed it. I did it to help them learn and understand the things that were good for them and the things that were not.

I am sure there have been many times in your life when friends have disappointed you. Perhaps you are still bitter about it. The bitterness will poison your life, and it will not change the people who let you down. Only God can change people, and only if they will allow Him to do so.

There is no point in ruining your life over someone else's bad choices. I strongly encourage you to stop looking to people for approval and acceptance and instead, look to God. Remember, if you have accepted Jesus as your Savior and Lord, God accepts you just as you are. He will work with you all the days of your life to continually bring you into the fullness of what you can be with His help.

Give Away What You Want to Receive

A good way to start receiving what you want from others is to start giving it first. It is the biblical principle of "seedtime and harvest" on which God's kingdom operates.[8] To be successful and reap the benefits of Christianity, we must understand this principle.

God has a good life planned for you, but just like everyone else, you will have to learn how to operate in His ways. For example:

> God loves us first — He gives us love, and then we love Him in return.
>
> He wants us to love Him, but He gives first.
>
> If we want to receive acceptance and unconditional love from others, we must begin giving to others what we want them to give to us.

Give mercy to others, and you will begin to reap mercy in relationships. Mercy is better than judgment:

> **Do not judge and criticize and condemn others, so that you may**

not be judged and criticized and condemned yourselves.

For just as you judge and criticize and condemn others, you will be judged and criticized and condemned, and in accordance with the measure you [use to] deal out to others, it will be dealt out again to you.

Matthew 7:1,2

Blessed are the merciful: for they shall obtain mercy.

Matthew 5:7 KJV

We usually want everyone to give to us and, in fact, we get angry when they don't.

God's ways are the exact opposite of man's ways.[9] The good news is, God's ways work, and man's don't.

Do things God's way, and you will have a great life. You will learn His ways as you spend personal time with Him, talking to Him as you would a good friend and reading His Word on a regular basis. Also, find someone who is really blessed and happy, and watch how that person lives. Don't follow miserable people. If you do, you will end up just like them. Choose your friends carefully — they have an effect on you. Form a habit of being good and kind to others, and you will be a happy person.

We spend too much of our time worrying about how others treat us. We should be concerned about how we are treating them. Remember — first give away what you want to receive. Any farmer knows that he will never reap a harvest without first sowing seed.

Begin today to be as radical about giving to others as you want them to be in giving to you!

If you want unconditional love, mercy and respect, begin giving it to others.

Don't fall into the trap of self-pity, being resentful toward those who don't meet your needs. Look to God to meet your needs and ask Him to use you to help someone else.

two

Emotional Pain and Disappointment

know that many of the young people who read this book are hurting emotionally. You may be one of them. You may have hurts that you have not shared with anyone.

In fact, many times when we are hurting, we won't admit it even to ourselves.

For years I was hurting really badly due to being sexually abused from the time I was a young child until I left home when I was eighteen. But I acted as if I really had things all together in my life. Most people would have never known or could not have even imagined what I was going through in my home life. It is amazing how good we get at hiding our pain.

> *Heal me, O Lord, and I shall be healed; save me, and I shall be saved. . . .*
> *Jeremiah 17:14*

If you are going through emotional pain and disappointment with life and people, I strongly encourage you to be honest with yourself and begin to talk to God about it. He really wants to help you. You can talk to God about absolutely anything — He understands all you go through in life.

You may even be in a situation similar to mine where you are being sexually abused. I encourage you to talk to someone you trust — your school guidance counselor, or youth pastor — or look in the yellow pages for a teen hot line, or do some online searching for a web site on the Internet for teen organizations that offer help, etc. The bottom line is, <u>don't wait</u>. Do whatever you feel God is leading you to do to get help immediately.

Emotional pain is one of the most devastating things that any of us must face and learn to deal with. We learn in the Bible that God heals **the brokenhearted.** (Isaiah 61:1.) He exchanges our hurts and pain for blessings if we give them to Him. He gives us . . . **beauty for ashes, the oil of joy for mourning, the garment of**

praise for the spirit of heaviness... (v. 3 KJV). God cares about how you feel.

Don't keep your hurts hidden. If you do, they will get deeper and deeper and do more and more damage to your personality.

For many years I refused to face the issues in my life. When I finally did face them, it took many more years to overcome the problems that had developed in my personality.

If you are running from reality, hiding from issues that need to be dealt with, I strongly encourage you to stop and begin right now to face your problems. The longer you put it off, the longer you will be in bondage and pain.

Being healed emotionally is painful, but at least it is a type of pain that leads somewhere positive if we turn to God for help with it. It hurts because we usually have to talk about and deal with things that have been buried within us for a long time.

God will draw things out of you at the right time — just open up to Him and tell Him you want to be made completely whole.

Living a Life of Pretense

Are you living a lie, a life of pretense? Are you doing things that you really don't want to do just to feel like part of a group or to be popular?

I know all about living a lie, and I also know from experience what it ultimately does to us. It is very damaging to our personality.

Because I felt abnormal due to the sexual abuse I was enduring at home, I was always a loner. Although I had some friends, they were very few and I always kept them at a distance. When any of them asked for my home phone number, I had to find some way not to give it to them because I got in trouble from my father when I received phone calls. He was very jealous of me and did not want me to have any friends. If you're lonely, I know how you feel.

My life consisted of trying to survive, of dodging people and situations that would uncover the horrible truth of what was going on in my life. I had to pretend with everyone — my father, my mother, my relatives, my teachers and my school acquaintances.

I was not allowed to participate in any social activities at school. When asked why I was not going to a certain football or basketball game, I always had to tell a lie to cover the truth.

Unbelievable numbers of people live in pretense in our society today. Parents pretend their marriage is fine when their behavior behind closed doors proves otherwise. Children watch the "pretend life" that Mom and Dad live and learn from their role models to live the same way.

We all pretend that things don't bother us that really do. We pretend that we are not hurt when we are, that we don't have needs when we do, that we are strong when we are weak — and the list goes on and on.

In my own life I have discovered that trying to hide something is much harder than bringing it out into the open.

We are, however, afraid of being vulnerable. Honesty makes us vulnerable to rejection or disapproval, so we try to pretend that we are whatever people want us to be. We do this to avoid facing and dealing with the pain of rejection or disapproval that can come from being truly honest with ourselves and others.

Being honest is not something to avoid; it will release you from the chains of emotional bondage. Begin right now to face the things that bother you and, with God's help, deal with them. It will keep you from wasting some of the most precious years of your life and living a life of disappointment.

Making Wrong Things Right

Has your life been a big disappointment up until now? That can change! No matter how others have treated you, be determined not to let their opinions and actions determine your worth and value as a person. Remember, God loves you, and you are precious in His sight. You are a valuable person, and God has a good plan for your life.

Have people disappointed you, perhaps even people you should have been able to trust and turn to at any time? Don't let your past dictate your future. Don't withdraw from life and intimate relationships because you have been disappointed in the past. Put your trust in God and ask Him to lead you to the right friends.

Even if your own family has disappointed and rejected you, God welcomes you into His family. His Word states that He adopts us as His own:

> **Although my father and my mother have forsaken me, yet the Lord will take me up [adopt me as His child].**
>
> **Psalm 27:10**

As you turn your life over to God, you will find Him bringing justice to you. He delights in taking wrong things and making them right. He works good out of what Satan and others intend for harm. (Genesis 50:20.)

I have an absolutely awesome life now, and yet I suffered horribly all of my teenage years. When I was twenty-three years old, I remember thinking that I had never been happy in my life. I prayed and asked God to send someone into my life who would really love me and let me be happy.

God has done much more than I even asked, and He will do the same thing for you.[1] He will take all of the wrong things done to you and work them out for good as you trust Him and His Word.

God Keeps His Promises

The Bible is God's book of guidelines on how to live a successful, outrageously wonderful life. Every issue we will ever face in life is covered somewhere in the Bible. It is filled with wisdom for everyday living.

God does not play guessing games with us. He is very plain in His Word about what He likes and does not like, what He approves of and does not approve of, what works and what does not work. When He promises something, He always does what He says He will do. This is something we are not accustomed to with people.

Be Patient with God — and with Yourself

The Holy Spirit is referred to in the Bible as **the Comforter.** He (the Spirit of God) comes to dwell inside the heart or spirit of believers — those of us who have made Jesus our Savior — where He ministers to us as individuals.[2] In other words, Jesus is living in your heart as a believer in Him, and He wants to comfort you when you are hurting through the indwelling Holy Spirit.

God is aware of everything that has ever happened to you in life. Even the very hairs on your head have been counted by Him.[3] When you turn to Him for help, He will begin to heal your emotions from the hurts and disappointments you have experienced. This healing is a process and will take some time. Little by little things will improve. Don't give up! You will begin to feel better about yourself and life in general. You will learn to trust people and yet be wise about who you should open up to and who you shouldn't.

During this process of healing, be patient with God and with yourself. Don't expect everything to be fixed overnight. Many people make this mistake and end up backsliding into old ways and lifestyles. They have been disappointed so many times in life, they begin to think that Christianity is a big disappointment also. The mistake they make is "trying" to live the Christian life instead of letting God live it through them.

By His Power

The mystery which has been hidden from ages and from generations, but now has been revealed to His saints.

. . . which is Christ in you, the hope of glory.

Colossians 1:26,27 NKJV

As we pray and ask God to help us, He does through us, by His power, what we cannot do on our own.

With many people it is, "God helps those who help themselves." With God, it is, **. . . Not by might, nor by power, but by My Spirit. . . , says the Lord of hosts** (Zechariah 4:6).

James 4:2 KJV states that we have not because we ask not. When we are in need of help, strength, wisdom, etc., we can ask God for it, and He will give us what we need.

I always say that God does not throw us the
football and then expect us to make the touchdown by
ourselves. After we are born again totally as an act of
God's mercy and grace, He does not expect us to live the
rest of our life without the same mercy and grace. He
knows that we need His help all the way through life. He
will help you with homework assignments, tests, decisions, finding a job, even fixing your hair. Actually, His
Word states in John 15:5, . . . **apart from Me [cut off
from vital union with Me] you can do nothing.** This
is a good lesson to learn early in our walk with God.

God has begun a good work in you, and He will
bring it to its finish. (Philippians 1:6.) You may feel thousands of times like nothing is changing in you or in your
life, but that is absolutely not true.

Our lives can get into such messes that correcting
them is like dismantling a mountain of hay one straw at a
time. We are very intricate beings. Our emotional makeup
can be quite complicated.

It is vital for you to believe every step of the way that God is working in you and that you will like the end result.

Surrender yourself to God for healing in every area of life. With His help, you can be set free from emotional hurts and disappointments to pursue the wonderful, happy, blessed life He has in mind for you!

Finish in Style

God wants to do a thorough work in us, to make us complete and whole. He can do that only if we allow Him to do so.

For most of my life I felt fragmented, pulled in all directions, like a broken vessel that had been shattered into pieces. I hurt mentally, emotionally, physically, spiritually, socially, financially and every other way a person can be hurt.

Over the years God has worked in me, and He has totally healed me. I am emotionally stable. I enjoy a peaceful mind. I have lots of joy, good friends and a great family. I am spiritually alive and have a wonderful relationship with God. I enjoy prosperity and good health. My beginning was not very pretty, but I am finishing in style.

Perhaps your beginning has not been very pretty either. If so, let my testimony concerning the goodness of God encourage you to believe that He will do the same thing for you that He has done for me.

God is no respecter of persons.[4] He loves us all the same. What He does for one of us, He will do for all of us.

Actually, God is like a life preserver for someone who is out in the middle of the ocean and doesn't know how to swim. You may feel like you're drowning in your circumstances, but you can trust yourself into His care. As you do, He will get into gear to help you and work out His good plan in your life.

three

Confronting Fear

Fear brings torment into our lives, but fear is not from God. Our enemy Satan comes to kill, steal and destroy, but Jesus came that we might **have and enjoy life** (John 10:10). None of us can enjoy life when we are fearful. We should be bold and courageous, not fearful and timid. As we will see later, this boldness and courage come from our relationship with God.

> *For God has not given us a spirit of fear, but of power and of love and of a sound mind.*
>
> *2 Timothy 1:7 NKJV*

You may have a quiet personality, or not be real aggressive, and that is okay. But you don't have to be afraid of life, letting others push you around and being too timid to stand up to situations and people that need to be confronted.

Satan starts very early, even while we are still babies, trying to build a stronghold of fear in our mind and emotions.

Of course, everyone has a normal, healthy fear, the kind of fear that warns us about things like looking both ways before crossing the street in the middle of oncoming traffic. But I am talking about a spirit of fear that holds many people in bondage.

I once looked up phobias (fears) in the encyclopedia, and the list seemed unending. People are afraid of everything from A to Z — animals, water, heights, bugs, dirt, people, death, lack, loneliness, driving a car, going out at night, the dark, failure, rejection and abandonment. Some are even afraid of success.

Fear keeps us trapped in a narrow lifestyle, and all the while God has this great big wonderful life planned for us. It grieves Him when we miss out on what He has provided for us through Jesus Christ.

Fear will not go away; it must be confronted. The word <u>fear</u> in the simplest form means to take flight or to run from.[1] <u>We are not in fear when we feel fear; we are in fear when we give in to the feelings of fear</u>.

Fear can cause shaking, trembling, sweating, a dry mouth, an overactive bladder, a wringing of the hands and several other symptoms. Fear can also cause us to make irrational decisions and take actions that we regret later. Don't be so afraid of losing your friends that you let them convince you to do things you don't feel right about.

We can learn to act on God's Word rather than react to the feelings of fear. In His Word, the Lord tells us, **Fear not, for I am with you...** (Isaiah 41:10 NKJV).

God is with us to help us. As a matter of fact, the Holy Spirit is referred to as **the Helper** as well as **the Comforter.** He is always standing by, even though He is unseen, ready to come to our aid in any situation.

<u>You no longer need to be controlled and driven by fear</u>.

When you find yourself being attacked by fear, call upon the power of God to strengthen you and enable you to stand against it. You no longer have to fight your battles alone; God wants to help you. Perhaps nobody else with pure motives has ever wanted to help you, but God does. Remember, He loves you and wants to help you live a good life.

Live the Good Life

Fear is not part of the good life God has planned for each of us. He won't remove all the feelings of fear that Satan brings against us, but He will make us able to confront our fears and begin to overcome them one by one.

The way we overcome things is by going through them. Confronting issues may be difficult, but it is necessary in order to conquer them. Once we are on the other side of a problem, we have gained experience as a result of what we have gone through. We can then use that experience to help others who are going through a similar problem. Actually, this is one way that God takes what Satan and others mean for our harm and works it out for good, as the Bible says He will.

Don't live a narrow life ruled by fears of all kinds. As situations come up, and you have an opportunity to bow to fear or confront it, ask God for help and start confronting. Do things afraid, if you have to, but do the things you want and need to do in life. Each time you do them, the feelings of fear will be weaker and weaker until it finally loses its control over you.

God has all the answers to all your problems. The world does not have your answers; God does!

We are often afraid of things that have happened to us previously.

A person who has been raped might be afraid of the same thing happening again. Someone who has had difficulty learning in school will probably be afraid of taking tests because they are an indication of what one truly knows. People who have failed at something in the past may be so afraid of failing again that they never step out and try anything. Don't allow that to happen to you. Abraham Lincoln lost several elections before he was elected president of the United States.

In the Bible a man who was suffering from the attacks of Satan cried out, ... **the thing which I greatly fear comes upon me, and that of which I am afraid befalls me** (Job 3:25). Just as faith has the ability to draw the blessings of God into our life, fear has the ability to draw bad things from Satan into our life.

As you have already seen, fear is only a feeling that Satan uses to try to keep you from fulfilling your destiny. He knows that if you grab hold of fear, you let go of your trust in God and open the door to his attack. Everybody feels fear at times; that is not the problem. It is what you do with fear that determines your outcome.

In the next section, you will see that Satan tries to use fear to keep you from progressing, but remember, fear cannot affect you if you don't give into the feeling and allow it to control you.

Satan Is Your Enemy

For we are not fighting against human beings but against the wicked spiritual forces in the heavenly world, the rulers, authorities, and cosmic powers of this dark age.

Ephesians 6:12 TEV

I have mentioned Satan several times in this book, and I want to make sure you realize he is your enemy.

Satan was an angel created by God. He rebelled against God and was kicked out of heaven.[2] He was created with great power and authority and still has that power over those who listen to him. He is a liar and a deceiver and seeks to totally destroy lives.[3] He hates God and everything He stands for; he also hates anyone who serves God.

Satan deceived Adam and Eve, who were the first human beings God created.[4] He tempted them to disobey God. Because they listened to him instead of to God, they lost a great deal of blessings.[5]

Satan thought he had destroyed God's man, but God had a plan of redemption. He would send His own Son Jesus into the world to pay for the sins of man.[6] Those who believed in God's plan to save them through Jesus would regain the original authority they were destined to have.

Satan has no authority over those who believe in Jesus Christ as Savior and Lord unless they are deceived into thinking they should fear him.

Many people are deceived about Satan. They think he is a cartoon character, someone who wears a red suit, carries a pitchfork and appears on Halloween and in spooky movies. They don't realize that he is real and is the one behind all their hurt and the devastating things that have happened to them in life. Often people blame God for their troubles, while not even being aware that Satan is their true enemy.

Many young people today are being lured into Satanism. They are being told they will have power if they serve Satan. Satan may give these teenagers power for a period of time, but when he is finished using them for his own purposes, they will be left an empty shell of what a person should be.

Satan uses people and then throws them away as trash, but you don't have to be one of those people. Beware of anyone who tries to lure you into Satanism or witchcraft. No matter how much they tell you it has helped them and given them power, believe me, it is not the true help and power God wants you to have.

It is Satan who brings fear into our life; he uses it to prevent our progress. Satan hates progress of any kind. He wants everything to be stagnant and dead. But Jesus said that He came into the world that we might have life — not a life filled with fear, but the abundant life He died on the cross to give us.[7]

Life is about progress. We are born and we grow; we learn and expand our knowledge; we step out into new areas and try new things; we succeed and we fail; we learn some more and try again. We are always learning about many things: relationships, God, what is really important in life, who to trust, what produces joy and what does not. Even our relationship with God is progressive — we get to know Him by spending time with Him, studying His Word and experiencing His faithfulness.

Satan hates progress, and he opposes it vehemently. As we have seen, he uses fear to prevent it.

The only acceptable attitude to take toward fear is, *I will not fear!* Make up your mind that you are not

going to live in fear, that you are going to enjoy the fullness of life that can only be experienced by living boldly.

"Fear Not" People's Opinions of You

The fear of man brings a snare,

but whoever leans on, trusts in, and

puts his confidence in the Lord is

safe and set on high.

Proverbs 29:25

Possibly the greatest fear we face in life is the fear
of man. It seems to affect everyone in some way.

I know that teenagers deal with many of the
same problems that adults do and that fear of what
others will think, say and do is one of the greatest fears
they have to face.

How many times do you say yes to other people
when really you want to say no? Why do you do it? Isn't it
because you are afraid of rejection, judgment or criticism?

Take a stand! You may feel like you're swimming
upstream and everyone else is floating downstream, and
they're saying to you, "Come on with us. You're going the

wrong way!" But don't allow others to run or ruin your life. You only have one life to live, and you should live it according to your conscience and convictions, not someone else's.

If your friends are not interested in going to heaven with you, refuse to go to hell with them!

Most of the people who try to control and manipulate you will drop you like a hot potato if their relationship with you no longer benefits them.

A manipulator is someone who tries to sway or give direction to another person shrewdly or deviously for personal gain.[8] In other words, manipulators are those who try to talk you into doing things the way they think you should do them. They may even tell you that what they are asking you to do is for your own good. The truth is, such people never have your best interest in mind at all. They just want to use you to get their own way.

I have found that people often try to talk others into doing the things they are doing just so they will feel secure about their own choices and decisions.

For example, suppose I want to cut my hair in a new style that is just becoming popular, but I don't have the courage to be different. If I can talk a friend into getting the same haircut, it will make me feel more secure because I will not be the only one with the new and perhaps attention-grabbing hairstyle. If people don't like it, at least there will be two of us to console each other.

There are times to take advice and times not to take advice, and we must learn to discern the difference. Not taking advice when we truly need to can lead us into great trouble and even defeat. Proud people often end up defeated. The Bible says, **Pride goes before destruction. . .** (Proverbs 16:18). Likewise, taking advice when that advice is incorrect or untimely can also lead to much heartache and personal pain.

Don't be rebellious toward authority, but remember that proper authority will not try to control you, dominate you or manipulate your every move and decision. People who genuinely care about you will want to help you fulfill your dreams and will back you up in your decisions (unless, of course, those decisions are immoral and ungodly).

If people are truly your friends, they will encourage you to be led by your own convictions, to do what you believe is right for you. Even though they may be disappointed, if you feel you cannot do what they suggest, they are understanding and give you the freedom to make your own decisions.

There is no such thing as a good relationship without freedom and liberty for all parties involved.

One time I wanted my daughter to go shopping with me. At first she said yes, but a little later she said, "My heart tells me I had better stay home with my family tonight." I did not ignore her feelings and push her and try to talk her into going with me. Even though I really wanted her to go, I had a stronger desire for her to follow what was right for her than what was right for me.

That is true love.

Don't Live Someone Else's Life — Live Yours!

Actually, the term for what I have been talking about is "peer pressure." It refers to being pressured by those whom we admire and whose approval we desire.

Everyone wants to be part of the most popular group at school, date the guys or girls everyone looks up to, get phone calls and invitations, be included in what is going on, etc.

We all want that, but often Satan uses our strong desires for acceptance against us. He leads us into adopting a lifestyle of compromise and mediocrity just so we can have the approval of our peers. That is a sad mistake to make.

The teenage years go by so quickly. You are only that age for a short time. But when those years are over, you have the rest of your life to live.

<u>The decisions you make today are building blocks for your future — make them carefully</u>.

When I was a teenager, everyone wanted to be "cool." That term may be out of date today, but whatever the acceptable term is now, the principle is the same. Most teens want to be "in," to be part of the crowd.

I encourage you to be careful about the price you pay for acceptance and popularity. Is it worth ruining your life by getting hooked on drugs just to be considered "cool"? Do you want to risk becoming an alcoholic by the time you are twenty-five just to be accepted by others? Do you want to go to prison or be killed in a violent street fight? Do you want to risk being a pregnant, unmarried teen just to be able to say you've had sex? Do you want the responsibility of being a father at age fifteen or sixteen? Is one moment of pleasure or acceptance worth the price you may have to pay for it later? Often people pay a high price for a cheap thrill.

Of course, we all like to think we can avoid the consequences. We all like to think we won't get caught, that we can smoke, drink or take drugs and not get "hooked."

These are lies from Satan. As we saw earlier, we reap what we sow. (Galatians 6:7,8.) If we make good choices based upon God's Word, we will reap the benefits. If we make bad choices, we will reap the consequences. It is deception to think that we will get away with making wrong choices and never have to pay the price for them. If you have already made some of these mistakes, God will help you. He is always willing to help us overcome the past and start a new life.

Before you go to school, to the mall or to any social gathering, be determined not to give in to peer pressure and compromise your lifestyle.

You don't have to dress like everyone else, do what they do, act like they act, talk like they talk or go where they go.

<u>Be an individual.</u>

God created you to be unique, one of a kind. You are special. You are a "Designer's original." With God's help, you can be all you were originally designed to be. It is not His will for you to struggle trying to be like everyone else. He may not lead you in the same direction He leads all of your friends, but if you follow His direction, you will see that it is right for you.

All of my daughter Sandra's friends went to college, but Sandra did not feel that God wanted her to go. It was a hard decision for her, and it was sometimes difficult for her when people would say, "What! You're not going to college? Well, why not?" She did not even know why not; she just knew she had no desire to go because she did not believe that was the direction for her to take.

As things turned out, she ended up working full time in the ministry with us and did not need a college education for her particular job. Now I am not saying that you don't need to go to college. But it seems Sandra was being led in the right direction for her life after all. If she had done what all her friends were doing, her decision would have been questionable at best.

Take some time to find out what is in your heart! Stop trying so hard to be accepted by your peers that you don't really enjoy your life. Don't live someone else's life — live yours!

Loneliness Is a State of Mind

Are you afraid of being lonely? I think there are times in life when we all are.

Eagles usually fly alone, but they appear majestic, not lonely.

If you want to do something great with your life, you may have to make decisions that will separate you from others temporarily. Don't be afraid of being alone.

You can be alone and not be lonely; likewise, you can be lonely and not be alone.

Loneliness comes from feeling unloved. As long as you know that God loves you, it is not necessary to feel lonely.

I love to spend time alone. Naturally, I would not want to be alone all the time, but there are worse things than spending a night at home alone.

Loneliness is a state of mind. It comes from wrong thinking that releases wrong emotions.

There is always something constructive you can do if you broaden your thinking. Finding constructive things to do keeps you from feeling lonely. It occupies your time, and soon the evening is over and it is another day. You could go to a big party and be with twenty-five people who really don't care about you and still feel lonely.

Going out with other people and engaging in shallow conversation and small talk to avoid being alone does not interest me. I would rather stay home and read a good book.

Ask yourself if the people you are around are saying anything worth listening to or are doing anything worth your involvement. If not, make some changes in your lifestyle.

Quiet Please!

Most people actually need more quiet time, more time alone, than they are getting. We live in a very busy society, and everyone seems to feel that every minute of their waking hours needs to be filled with something.

We are addicted to entertainment.

I remember as a teenager that normal living was going to school five days a week and doing chores and homework five nights a week. Baby-sitting on weekends was not uncommon. If we did something for entertainment occasionally, we enjoyed it, but we did not feel deprived if we were not entertained every night of the week.

After I graduated from high school and got married, I began to notice a real change in society. By the time I had my last child, it seemed that to most people entertainment had become a daily necessity rather than an occasional luxury.

Today we have entertained ourselves to such a degree that it is getting harder and harder to find something to do that actually seems fun. We have seen and done so much, and usually at such a young age, that now it all seems boring. An overabundance of anything can cause us to lose our appreciation for it.

When I was a child, a trip to Disney World would have been a dream, something we only saw on television. But today my children have been there so many times, they did not even want to go back the last time we mentioned it.

My point is that all this addiction to activity we have gotten into has given us the mistaken idea that staying home alone is a curse. It is, in fact, a blessing!

Make a decision right now that you are going to start confronting your fears and that fear of what people think about you is going to be on the top of your list. Say out loud, "I am not going to give in to peer pressure ever again. I am not going to compromise out of loneliness or fear of rejection. I am going to make my own decisions and follow my own heart."

Now stick to that decision. Spend a lot of quiet time just thinking about your future. Make some plans. Dream big dreams. Start praying about your future now, asking God to bless it and be involved in leading you toward it. He wants you to enjoy all that He has in store for you.

four

Overcoming Your Past

I do not consider, brethren, that I have captured and made it my own [yet]; but one thing I do [it is my one aspiration]: forgetting what lies behind and straining forward to what lies ahead,

I press on toward the goal to win the [supreme and heavenly] prize to which God in Christ Jesus is calling us upward.

Philippians 3:13,14

> *I press on toward the goal to win the [supreme and heavenly] prize....*
> *Philippians 3:14*

Are there things in your past that threaten your future, things of which you are ashamed? Have you made mistakes? Have you failed at something? Are there things in your parents' lives that embarrass you or of which you are ashamed?

To be honest, I think we all have some skeletons in our closet, things we wouldn't want anyone to know. The good news is that God already knows everything about your past and future, and He loves you anyway. More good news is that we are all in the same boat. You are not alone in having a past that you wish you did not have.

First, let me say that you can overcome the mistakes of the generation that raised you or is raising you.

Divorce is very prevalent today, but that does not mean that if you decide to get married when you are older, you have to get divorced at some point. Marriage can work and be wonderful.

By the way, God still approves of marriage, and He still disapproves of couples living together in sin. If your parents lived in sin, took drugs, were alcoholics, lived in poverty or did other things that brought pain into your life, that does not mean you cannot overcome it.

I was sexually, verbally, mentally and emotionally abused throughout my childhood and teenage years. My home was filled with violence, beatings, cursing, anger and alcohol. I grew up in a total state of fear. I was told I was no good and would never amount to anything. Yet in spite of all these things, I have a wonderful, joy-filled life today. Why? Because I made up my mind that I would overcome my past, and I asked God to help me do it.

Don't just sink into a pit and decide to stay there all of your life because of a past that was unsuitable.

God says we are to forget the past and press toward the future. His mercy is new every day, and every new day is actually an opportunity to have a fresh start in life.

Don't sit around and be depressed. Get up and do something about making some changes in the things you don't like.

If you had an abortion or a baby out of wedlock or were involved in some other kind of wrong behavior, God will forgive you. He is forgiving and long-suffering. If you are sincere in your sorrow about past mistakes, He is quick to forgive. If you disappointed your parents, you can rebuild your relationship with them. If they disappointed you, pray for them and look to the future, not the past. Don't be bitter about the past; let it be a tutor for your future.

One of the good things about past mistakes is that we have already gained valuable experience in what to do and what not to do; therefore, we don't have to make those same mistakes again.

In His Word, God encourages us to be overcomers.[1] In order to do that, we must have something to overcome.

<u>You can overcome your past!</u>

I really want you to believe that. Satan wants you to believe that it is too late, that you have made too many mistakes and that you are at a dead end. Remember, in God there are no dead ends; every day is a new beginning.

When I look back at how awful my childhood and teenage years were, I am absolutely amazed at how far I have come. One of the most important things I had to do to change my life was stop feeling sorry for myself.

Self-Pity Is a Dead-End Street

You can be pitiful if you want to, but self-pity will not open the door to powerful living. Self-pity is a dead-end street. It takes you nowhere except into a deeper pit of depression and despair. It causes you to turn in on yourself and see only what is wrong with your life. It is a very negative and destructive emotion.

For years I was plagued with self-pity over my past. Finally, I learned that although I could not do anything about my past, I could do a lot about my future.

Self-pity keeps you trapped in the things that have made you sad. You keep reliving them over and over again in your thinking.

Some people feel so sorry for themselves they begin to believe that life is not even worth living and so they contemplate suicide. Suicide is cowardly; it is the easy way out. Facing life is the challenge that God created us for.

Sometimes people hurt so badly for so long that they go over the edge mentally and commit suicide, but that was not the best answer for their life. God could have helped them if they had been willing to let Him do so. They could have had a wonderful life. They could have gotten over past mistakes and disappointments, but it takes hard work and an investment of time. Perhaps nobody ever told them they could overcome. Perhaps they felt so defeated they just gave up. But I want to make sure you don't become a statistic along with many other teens who are putting an end to their pain and confusion by committing suicide.

You Have a Lot to Live For!

For I know the thoughts and plans that I have for you, says the Lord, thoughts and plans for welfare and peace and not for evil, to give you hope in your final outcome.

Jeremiah 29:11

Don't sink into self-pity, but rise to right living and a bright future. Keep saying to yourself, "My future is so bright, I need sunglasses to look at it."

Remember, there are many promises in God's Word about overcoming. As we have already seen, God gives us His power to face and handle anything we need to deal with.

It is nice if you have someone to help you overcome your past problems, but even if you don't, you and God together are a powerful partnership that can conquer anything in life. Don't be impatient; just keep pressing forward. Remember, little by little you will overcome and begin enjoying a new life.

Don't feel defeated by past sins, mistakes or failures. When you and I ask God to forgive our sins, He also forgets them.[2] It is harder for us to forget them than for Him. We keep bringing up things from the past, while God wants to get on with the future. He is progressive; He is not looking back.

God has offered you a new life, a brand-new start, and your future has no room for your past mistakes and your sadness about them. No matter how bad you have been in the past, there are those who have been worse, and God loves them too.

It is easier to believe God loves other sinners than to believe He loves us — but I challenge you to start believing today! Wave goodbye to your past and expect good things to happen to you.

Forget the Past and Go Forward!

Jesus continually ministered to people with a sordid past. He said to the woman who was caught in the very act of adultery, **. . . go, and sin no more.**[3] The word "go" here indicates leaving the past and going forward. Jesus was saying to this woman, *Go forward, and don't make the same mistakes you made in the past.*

Jesus called many of His twelve disciples by telling them to leave what they were doing and follow Him. He was saying to them, *Whatever was in your past, leave it, and I will show you how to live life the right way.*

It is necessary to leave something in order to go on to something else. Some people's lives never go anywhere because they keep trying to drag the past into their future.

For many years I suffered terrible condemnation over my past, but I finally learned to let it go and go on. Each time I did something wrong, I persecuted myself for days on end by feeling bad, sad and guilty. I repented and asked God to forgive me, but I kept feeling guilty.

I am glad to say I am totally free from that method of handling my sins and errors. I get up every day and do the best I can. I repent for my mistakes when I make them and go on to the next day. That way, I make rapid progress; otherwise, I am just spinning my wheels and getting nowhere.

Being stuck in the past, whether it is the past from ten years ago or the past from yesterday, is just like being stuck in the mud. You may put out all kinds of effort and yet go nowhere. Why? Because God does not want you to drag your past into your future. He knows your past will poison it.

Your past is called the past because it has passed. There is only one thing you can do with your past — forget it! God has forgotten it, and so can you.

Romans 8:37 tells us that we are more than conquerors through Christ Who loves us. See yourself as a conqueror, an overcomer, not as someone defeated who can never get over the past. It may take some time to retrain your thinking into the future instead of the past, but you can do it — if you refuse to give up.

Everything Is Subject to Change — Except God

The Bible tells us that God does not change,[4] whether He is manifested in the form of the Father, His

Son Jesus or the Holy Spirit.[5] His Son Jesus, Who is the same as God, **is the same yesterday, today, and forever** (Hebrews 13:8 NKJV). He is called **the Rock**[6] because we can stand firm on Him and His Word and know for certain that He won't change His mind about loving us, forgiving us, helping us or anything else He has promised us in His Word.

God does not lie.[7] Honesty is part of Him; it is embedded in His character. In the Book of John, Jesus said that He is **the Truth** (John 14:6).

Everything else is subject to change, and we must accept that fact. Things and people around us are changing all the time. This is one of the reasons I know your future can change and not be like your past.

The promises of God are activated by believing in them.[8] You must believe that you can change, and so can your life. Say this out loud at least once a day: *Every day I get better and better in every way.*

The weather changes. People change. Commitments, appointments, careers, financial status, health — they are all subject to change. When things are good, they can get worse if we don't do what we should do to take care of them. We can be healthy and lose our health through neglecting our physical need for rest, exercise, good nourishing food and fun. We can have financial prosperity and through bad investments, overindulgence and other bad habits lose what we have and actually end up living in poverty.

Once we gain anything in life we must then maintain what we have gained.

A good relationship can be ruined and devastated by ignoring the responsibility side of relationships. How many failed marriages could have been saved if the couple had behaved toward one another after marriage the same way they did during courtship?

It is amazing and actually disgusting how often we do the right thing until we get what we want, and then don't do what we should to take care of it.

Taking care of what we have is part of maturity.

A child may be given lots of things and lose them all by not taking care of them. That is one reason children should be taught to work for what they want in life — if everything is handed to them by someone else, they may have difficulty appreciating what others have labored to get them.

Just as things can be good and get worse, they can also be bad and get better. If you are not satisfied with your life, locate the root of your dissatisfaction. You may be blaming others for it when, in actuality, you should make some changes yourself.

It is very easy to blame, blame, blame. We can spend our whole lives blaming, but it changes nothing. Taking ownership of our lives and being responsible for our actions — past, present and future — is the seed that must be sown if we want a different harvest to enjoy.

<u>Things can change!</u> You can change. Your circumstances, finances, health, education, career, friends — they can all change.

Other people who know you may have difficulty believing that you can ever change. Don't be influenced by their negative attitude.

When people we have been involved with have a negative record about us etched in their minds, they become discouraged and find it hard to believe in us. They don't want to be disappointed again.

But remember this: <u>No matter how many people don't believe in you, God does</u>. He actually has more faith that you can change than you do.

We frequently look at ourselves and think there is no hope of change, which is precisely what Satan wants. He wants us to be hopeless. But Romans 5:5 says that those who put their hope in God will never be disappointed or put to shame.

Don't allow yourself to be discouraged by the discouragement and unbelief of others.

In the Bible, God changed David from a shepherd boy into a king. But before David could ascend to the throne, he had to face many obstacles in life. One was a giant named Goliath, who was a Philistine warrior. Nobody else had been able to stand up to him due to fear, but David believed he could kill the giant. His family, the reigning king and everyone who heard his positive attitude tried to discourage him. They kept telling him what he was not: he wasn't old enough, he didn't have enough experience or the right armor and weapons. But David refused to be discouraged by their negativism. He encouraged himself by remembering past victories, times in his life when his back was against the wall, and with God's help, he overcame all the obstacles and defeated the giant Philistine.[9]

I encourage you to take the same attitude David did. Even if you cannot find one human being to encourage you and believe in you, believe in God and in His power in you to accomplish great things. Through God's power you can let go of the past and press toward the future. You can believe in the power of change. Always remember: <u>Everything is subject to change — except God Who never changes.</u>

As a matter of fact, you are changing right now as you read this book. You are getting new information inside you that will change your entire way of thinking and your whole outlook on life.

Picking Up the Pieces

Don't make the mistake of discarding everything from your past. Pick up the pieces and give them all to

God in prayer. You will be amazed what the Lord can do with fragments. He delights in recycling things and making unbelievable new things from the old.

You also have gained valuable experience from your past. You have learned some things that you probably don't want to relearn by going through them again. Take the wisdom you have gained and sow all the rest as seeds.

One time the operators of a television station broke their contract with us. They had been airing my program one day each week. Abruptly, without notice, they took it off the air. It was our number-one income-producing station, reaching millions of people. We had put a lot of money into airtime during the period we had been on that station while waiting to build a good viewing audience.

Sometimes stations wait until someone like me builds an audience for them. Then they change programming hoping to maintain the audience for what they want to show. They sell the time for more money to another person or company who wants to buy time. They sell it with a guaranteed audience that someone else like me has paid for and built up. This, of course, is cruel. It is also dishonest and very poor business ethics, but that is the way people are sometimes.

This situation really hurt me. I felt terribly wounded, so much so that I cried. It frustrated me because I could not do anything about it. I knew what had been done to me was wrong, but I just had to take it. Then I got angry and could feel bitterness getting rooted in my mind and emotions.

During this time God brought a great revelation to my heart: <u>Nobody can take anything from you if you are willing to give it and sow it as a seed</u>. I immediately knew what He was trying to show me because I under- stood the "seedtime and harvest principle" in the Bible. I could feel robbed, taken advantage of, angry and bitter, but none of that would change a thing. Or, I could release the situation to God, sow it as a seed and ask Him to bring a harvest of something better in my life.

I did release it, trusting God to be faithful to His Word. I felt so good inside after releasing that situation.

God cannot work in our situations unless we follow His ways. Although His ways are quite different from the world's ways, the fact is that His ways work and worldly ways don't.

About a year went by. Then one day a representative from the station that had taken us off the air called and asked us to go back on the air five times a week — and at a better time slot than we had had previously.

God brought justice! He always will, if we do things His way.

You might say about this situation that I was left with a broken dream. I picked up the pieces, gave them to God and He put them back together much better than before.

The same thing can happen to you as you offer God the pieces and fragments of your broken life. He specializes in fixing things that are broken. He heals broken hearts, broken marriages, broken relationships and broken dreams — He is the Great Physician!

No matter how good our life is, everything will not turn out as we desire. To be successful in life we must learn to continually let go of the past and go on to what lies ahead. It is a godly principle that we dare not ignore.

I know scores of people whose lives have been ruined by bitterness, resentment, hatred, regret, grief, sadness, depression, discouragement, hopelessness, etc. But, thank God, I also know thousands who have followed godly principles and are now enjoying life — and that **more abundantly** (John 10:10).

<u>And I believe that you can do the same thing</u>.

That's one of the reasons I have written this book — to prod you to move up to another level and get you unstuck not only from where you're at, but from where you've been!

five

Priorities in Relationships

You shall love the Lord your God with all your heart and with all your soul and with all your mind (intellect).

This is the great (most important, principal) and first commandment.

And a second is like it: You shall love your neighbor as [you do] yourself.

Matthew 22:37-39

Relationships are a major part of all of our lives. We cannot avoid them. God created us to need each other.

People who pretend not to need anyone in their life are only fooling themselves. These are usually individuals who have been hurt and are trying to avoid more emotional pain.

> *...You shall love the Lord your God....*
> *Matthew 22:37*

Relationships are vital, but they are one of the areas that can cause a lot of confusion. We need people, but they can be very difficult to deal with, to get along with and to know how to handle.

For example, we want people's approval of us and try hard to please everyone. Yet it seems that someone in our life is always displeased, and we are once again experiencing the pain of rejection. Or, it may seem that the only time people are happy with us is when we are doing what they want us to do. We want to share with others our deepest feelings and desires, our fondest dreams and goals, but we dare not for fear we will be ridiculed, rejected or even betrayed. And the sad truth is that many times we have been treated unfairly by those we trusted most.

Whatever your experience has been in the past, I want to assure you that you can have great relationships. But to do that, you have to set priorities and boundaries.

A priority is something of primary importance to us. To establish fulfilling and satisfying relationships, you must decide which ones are the most important to you, listing them in descending order. Doing that may help you make some interesting discoveries.

You may, for example, discover that you have been putting a lot of time into a relationship that is rather unimportant in the whole scope of things, while ignoring others that should be given a place of priority.

One evening after I had just finished a lengthy telephone conversation with a friend, my husband told me that he really got tired of sitting alone in the family room while I hung on the phone all night with my church friends. The particular woman I was talking with at the time was one with whom I usually visited by phone every evening. Today that woman is no longer even part of my life. I might add that she withdrew rather abruptly at a time when I was being falsely accused of some things and really needed her friendship. My husband, however, is still around. That incident made me realize that I should have been spending my time developing and nurturing my relationship with him instead of with someone who obviously did not really care about me anyway.

Based on that experience, let's look at some of the relationships in your life and try to establish a proper pattern of priorities among them.

God First

Who are you spending most of your time with? The Scripture quoted at the beginning of this chapter says that Person should be God. He should be first in your life.

None of our other relationships are solid until we put God first. That is because He is the cord that binds us together with each other. He is the foundation on which everything in our life must be built. Without Him, and what He teaches as our guidelines for relationships, we usually end up in strife with a trail of wounded feelings everywhere we look.

Put God first, and He will take care of everything else. What do I mean when I say put God first? Spend time talking to Him. Let Him be your Best Friend. Read His Word; it is His love letter to you. Read good books like this one that will help you be better at living for God and being the kind of person He has designed you to be. Talk about Him to your other friends.

We always talk about what is important to us. If you want to be successful in your other relationships, think about God and acknowledge Him and His Presence in everything you do.

Right Relationship with Your Parents

After God, the next relationship in your life that should be solid is your relationship with your parents.

Perhaps your parents have problems and are not doing their part to develop and nurture a right relationship with you. You cannot do anything about what others are not doing, but you can decide to do your part. God will bless you for it.

Friends are important, but I encourage you not to put your friends before your family. Most of the people you give your life to today won't even be around in a few more years, but your family will.

If you don't develop and nurture your relationships with your family members, you may be disappointed someday to discover that you need them, but if they are willing to help you at all, it will only be out of a sense of obligation, not out of love.

Our family is very close. When any member has a need, all the others are quick to run to meet that need. Sometimes we are so eager to support one another that it is almost ridiculous.

For example, the last time I was in the hospital, I went in at 6:00 A.M. for some outpatient procedures. My husband, whom I expected to go with me, did so. But besides Dave, all my children, most of their spouses, my brother and two of my best friends all went with me. We looked rather odd coming to the hospital at six o'clock in the morning in this large group. I am sure people must have thought that I had something really seriously wrong with me to draw this many people out that early. Actually, it was a minor surgical procedure, but my entire family insisted on being there.

The man who handled my registration asked if all those people were my family. When I said yes, he said, "That is really nice; we don't see much of that these days."

My family's decision to be there with my husband and me was based on the years we have had building good relationships and on the fact that we are always there for any of them when they need us.

Too often we expect something from others for which we have never sown seeds. If we want people to show love and concern for us, we must sow seeds by showing love and concern for them.

As a teenager, your family members may not seem very important right now, but actually they are one of the greatest assets you have. If they are not, then they should be.

As I have mentioned, your parents may not be doing their part with you, but someone in your family has to start doing the right thing at some time, and it may as well be you.

Romans 12:18 tells us, **If possible, as far as it depends on you, live at peace with everyone.** Some people don't want to be peaceful, but God is asking us to at least try. The normal attitude is, "If you treat me bad, I will treat you the same way." But once again we see that

God's way is just the opposite. He says, "Do unto others as you want them to do to you."[1] He does not say, "Do unto others what they do to you."

Don't be so angry with your parents if they don't seem to understand you. Believe me, when you have children of your own, things will have changed and you will probably not understand them either.

The things I wanted to do as a teenager seemed ridiculous to my parents, and the things my children wanted to do seemed ridiculous to me. I have learned over the years to be willing to change, but once we are set in our ways that is not easy.

I remember my mother-in-law getting angry with Dave and me because we bought a dishwasher. She felt that she had spent her life washing dishes by hand and that we should save our money and not provide that luxury for ourselves. She was a wonderful woman, but sometimes it was difficult for her to change. Later, all of her children had dishwashers — and she even got one.

As I have said, change is not easy, but it is necessary for progress.

The way you want to dress as a teenager may seem to be a point of contention with your parents. Just make sure you really want to dress in some particular style to express your own tastes and personality and not just because you want to be like everyone else in order to feel accepted or "in."

Make sure you are not acting out of rebellion. Try to find some middle ground where you can have what you want without putting your parents in a mental hospital in the process. Chances are they love you and want what is best for you, even though you may feel sure they don't know what that is.

Baggy pants and clothes purchased at the Goodwill store, bleached hair standing straight up or hair colored in vivid shades of red, purple or green were the style when our younger son Dan was a teenager and are actually still the style as I write this book. Hopefully, by the time you read it, things will have changed — though they will probably not be any more pleasing or appealing to most adults than the teenage styles are now. But if not,

I have learned that how people dress does not always indicate what kind of people they are.

We adults have a bad habit of judging young people based on what we thought was right for us in our youth. Judging teens by how they dress or fix their hair (or often don't fix their hair) is not God's way. He has said plainly that we cannot judge people's heart by their exterior appearance.[2]

Today it is the style for men not to shave their face completely but to leave some whiskers showing, so they will have what is called the "rugged look." Of course, I don't like this style, but my children say they do.

As adults, it is hard for us to understand how anybody could like something we don't. But since that happens all the time, I have decided to get used to not liking everything people do, but liking the people anyway. I suggest that you adopt the same attitude.

If you want your parents to be patient with you, start sowing seeds by being patient with them. Realize that some of the changes in every generation are always hard on those who are still around from the previous generation.

When our son Dan was a teenager, he really wanted to get a tattoo, and I really did not want him to get one because I thought he might regret it later in life. We had many conversations about it. Finally, he did get some, but one of them is my name in Chinese, so I couldn't be too upset. There have been other things he wanted to do but refrained from just to honor me. It would be different if I were trying to run every aspect of his life, always coming against everything he wanted to do. But that is not the case.

You may find that it will go a long way in your relationship with your parents if you will give in (with a smile) sometimes just to honor them. Don't try so hard to be like all of your friends that you alienate your family.

If you have a tattoo, or even several tattoos, don't feel that I am judging you critically because I said I did not want my son to have one. That is simply my personal preference. You are free to do what your heart leads you to do.

I told my son that the only tattoo he could have was one that said, "I love my mom." It actually became a big joke between us.

Later, I had my eyebrows permanently put on because they were so thin and short. When Dan found out that it was done by tattooing, he said that I owed him two tattoos.

Believe it or not, you can have fun with your parents, and they can lighten up and have fun with you.

You may feel that your parents and other adults treat you as if you are from outer space. The truth is that as an adult I don't always feel accepted as I am by teenagers, just as you may not always feel accepted as you are by adults. Once again, you may be expecting something from your parents that you are not willing to give them. I don't always like my son's clothes or choice of hairstyle, but he doesn't always like mine either, and, I might add, he is not shy about verbalizing his opinion. We voice opinions but don't try to control one another.

I don't believe that parents are always right and teens are always wrong. Actually, I firmly believe it usually takes two parties to have a problem. But I am saying that more understanding from both sides is what is needed. We can learn from each other.

We must be careful about heart attitudes. We can allow an attitude to get in us that always leaks through into our behavior with others. If we want other people to treat us right, then we must treat them right. We start treating them right by having right thoughts about them.

Instead of thinking, *My parents don't understand me,* try thinking, *My parents don't understand me, but I believe they love me and are doing the best they can for me.*

Your parents may also need to change their thinking toward you. They may need to stop thinking negative, downgrading and accusing thoughts about you.

In either case, we would all do well to remember that <u>love always believes the best of people</u>.

If all of us, teenagers and adults, think better thoughts about each other, we will get along better with one another. Regardless of our age, we can all benefit by realizing (or remembering) that growing up is difficult. The teenage years are a time when young people experience a lot of conflicting emotions. It can be a time of pressure from peers, parents and teachers. Teenagers need love and understanding, not judgment and criticism.

Relationships with Friends

You will have a lot of different relationships with different people. You may enjoy some very close relationships with a few, but that will not be the case with everyone you know.

Even Jesus seemed to be closer to Peter, James and John than He was to the other nine disciples. However, I don't believe He slighted any of them or made any of them feel left out or rejected. He loved them all the same with the love of God that was in Him; but for some reason His relationship with Peter, James and John seemed a little closer. Perhaps they responded better to Him than some of the others, and it was more natural for Him to respond back.

Love can be given, but it also must be received. I have tried at times to be friendly with people who did not return my gestures, and no relationship ever formed. I did not dislike them, but I had to move on to relationships that included give and take, not just take and take with no giving back.

You cannot be best friends with everybody. I encourage you to let God develop what I call "divine connections" in your life.

We are often guilty of trying to choose those with whom we want to be friends and sometimes get hurt in the process. Our motives for our choices are not always pure either. We may want to be friends with certain people because they are popular or because we see them as a doorway to what we want. They may know someone we want to know or have something we would like to have. These are wrong motives on which to try to build a friendship.

Make sure your motives are pure as you select your friends. Never try to use people to get something you desire. If you will pray about your friendships and let God lead you in making them, He will bring you into relationship naturally and easily with the people who are right for you.

If you are in relationship with someone right now with whom you are uncomfortable, I suggest you start moving out of the relationship. It can be done gradually or in such a way that the person doesn't get hurt. If you don't follow your heart, you may end up in trouble.

Relationships are a great area in which to pray for discernment. Some people may seem to have it all together and look like the perfect ones to be friends with, but down deep inside they may have serious problems that will cause you problems if you get involved with them. Discernment is not just "skin deep." It sees beyond the surface and discerns the true character of people.

If you are in relationship with someone who keeps trying to tempt you to do things that you know are wrong — get away from that person! You must guard and protect yourself. Don't let people control you or use you.

If you have accepted Jesus as your Savior, and your friends are making fun of you because of it, don't allow them to get you to change your mind about your decision. You might tell them what I heard one young woman tell her boyfriend who was trying to get her to give up her relationship with Jesus: <u>If you won't go to heaven with me, I won't go to hell with you.</u> I think that statement says it all.

Always remember, when you make right choices that are going to help you go forward, Satan will provide someone through whom he will try to pressure you into going back where you came from. This is called backsliding.

Don't go to jail for someone else. Don't get hooked on drugs for someone else. Don't give up your virginity for someone else.

<u>Don't get talked into doing anything you don't want to do!</u>

What about your real friends? What kind of priority should you set in your relationship with them? You obviously need to spend good quality time with them. You need to be available for them when they need you — unless, of course, their needs are out of balance.

Some people are so needy they suffocate us. The Bible encourages us not to get "entangled" with people or things that will draw us off our intended course.

Help your friends all you can. Pray for them. Do things with them. Talk to them on the telephone. But don't get "entangled" with them or their problems.

There is a difference between entanglement and balanced relationships within proper priorities and boundaries. If you don't have proper boundaries in relationships, you will almost always get out of balance and end up ruining what could have been a great relationship if it had been kept in balance.

I once had a friend who had a lot of personal problems. She was never very happy, and her constant unhappiness was conflicting with my happiness. She became angry when things did not go her way, and I found myself being controlled by her. I was doing lots of things I did not want to do just to keep the peace. I should have confronted her and learned to say no, but my own fears hindered me from doing what was right.

In order to set boundaries, we have to learn when to say no and when to say yes. If we always say yes even when our heart is saying no, then we have no boundaries, and without boundaries we are not protected.

This friend wanted to be with me all the time, but her sadness and depression began to drag me down. I felt that I was always trying to "prop her up" or "fix her problem."

<u>People cannot give you their problems if you refuse to take them.</u>

I wanted to help this woman, but the truth was that her problems were perpetual. I really could not help her because she needed an attitude change. I allowed myself to become entangled in her problems, and it basically ruined our relationship. If I had set some boundaries in the beginning, we might still be friends today.

Boundaries are good things. They give us safe places in which to live. A life without boundaries will ultimately end in disaster.

All relationships should have boundaries, including the parent-child relationship. We have already discussed this kind of realtionship, but one more point needs to be made in regard to boundaries. Parents must begin releasing authority and responsibility to their children as they grow toward adulthood. Sometimes children want authority without responsibility, and sometimes parents want to give children responsibility but no authority to make any of their own decisions. Both of these unbalanced scenarios are wrong.

Parents should not expect their children to be responsible to obey them if they never release any authority to them. Good behavior should always be rewarded with an increase in privileges.

This same principle holds true in other relationships such as the relationship between employer and employee and between God and the believer. The believer's relationship with God is another kind of relationship we have already talked about, but I want to point out that it also has boundaries. God releases both authority and responsibility. Unless the believer is willing to take both, he can have neither.

As believers, God is our Friend (among other things). Along with that friendship comes responsibility; we are responsible for walking in obedience to Him.[3] As we do so, He releases authority to us.

I realize your friends are a very important part of your life. I encourage you to have lots of wonderful relationships. Just be wise not to allow them to get out of balance. Don't spend so much time with your friends that you have no time for God or family.

You have lots of years left to live; therefore, you don't have to try to do all your living right now and act as if you are almost out of time.

I believe the teenage years should be some of the best in your life, years you can look back on with enjoyment.

I regret to say mine were a nightmare. I had no real friends. I was very lonely, enduring abuse and living in a home that was very dysfunctional.

I pray this is not the case with you. But even if things in your life are not up to par, don't try to make up for it through relationships with friends who cause you to get all your other priorities out of balance.

According to Ecclesiastes 3:1-8 NIV, there is a time for everything in life. I believe there is a time to be with people and a time to be alone, a time to build relationships and a time to walk away from some of them.

There is a time to be with friends, but not during the time you should be with God or with family.

Your Relationship with Yourself

Perhaps it never occurred to you that you have a relationship with yourself. Actually, you spend more time with yourself than with anyone else. If you think about it, you literally never get away from yourself — so you had better like yourself.

Today in our ministry and in our own youth outreach called <u>Rage Against Destruction</u>, we deal with many teens who are filled with self-hatred, self-rejection and deep-rooted shame. Many of them are self-abusers and some are even suicidal. Much of the time, addiction to drugs and alcohol, eating disorders like bulimia and anorexia, and even premarital sex are attempts to find fulfillment, love and acceptance. Those who engage in these kinds of activities don't know the love of God, and they don't love themselves in a balanced way.

We are not supposed to love ourselves selfishly, mistreating others in order to get our own way, but we do need to love ourselves properly. Sometimes we spend so much time comparing ourselves with others and competing with them that we never get to know ourselves.

You have tremendous worth and value. In fact, you are a great person to get to know. But like everyone else, you have strengths and weaknesses. I encourage you not to major on your weaknesses but to turn them over to Jesus and let Him be strong through them. His strength is made perfect through our weakness.[4]

Learn to get along with yourself. If you don't, you will always have difficulty getting along with others.

For many years I could not seem to maintain a good relationship with anyone, and I kept blaming everyone else for it. I thought if they would change, then we could get along. I finally learned from the Lord that my real problem was that I was not getting along with myself.

If we don't get along with ourselves, we won't get along with anyone else either.

When you meet someone who seems to hate everyone and everything, you can be sure that person's self-image is rooted in self-hatred.

It may be new to you to think that you have a relationship with yourself, but it is a very important relationship, one that can cause lots of other problems if it isn't healthy. Like every other relationship, getting to know yourself will take time. Therefore, you must give it a place of priority in your life.

Be honest with yourself about your strengths and weaknesses. Think about what <u>you</u> like and dislike. Don't determine your worth by how other people view you, respond to you or treat you.

We always assume that we have something wrong with us if someone rejects us, but that may not be true — the other person could be the one with the problem.

Satan convinced me that I had something wrong with me because my father was sexually abusing me, but I realize now that a small child is not the perpetrator in a case of incest. I suffered self-hatred for years and, therefore, had a bad relationship with myself because I believed Satan's lies.

What lies are you believing about yourself? What is it that you don't like about yourself — your level of intelligence, your looks, your body size, your talents and abilities, your standing in society, your family background?

We all have things about ourselves we would like to change. Some of the things you don't like about yourself, however, may be things that are not going to change. You may have to accept them and realize they are not the big deal you may be making them out to be.

Having one pimple on your cheek does not ruin your looks. Everyone has flaws; we hardly notice other people's, but we sit and stare at our own. Some of the things that you think are your greatest flaws may be the very things that God will use the most.

I always hated my deep voice. I thought it sounded more like a man than a woman. I wanted a soft, sweet voice. I was (and still am) often thought to be a man when answering the phone, unless the person on the other end of the line knows me really well. I hated my voice and was insecure about it, but God is using it worldwide today.

Who would have ever thought that God gave me a unique voice, not a weird voice as Satan would have had me believe, and that He gave it to me so it would be distinct, recognizable and attention getting?

Don't be too quick to decide what things about yourself are usable or unusable. God may surprise you.

God does not make junk, and He made you. As the psalmist said of himself, God formed you in your mother's womb with His very own hands. (Psalm 139:13.) You were an intricate, special project, and you should accept yourself as such, even with your faults, and then give your entire self to God. He loves you. Receive His love, and love yourself in a balanced way. Then you will be able to reach out to others with love and acceptance. As you learn to trust God, He will help you make the changes in yourself that are really necessary.

Perhaps you don't like your body size. I had that problem in my life. I was always chunky. As a teenager I was just pudgy enough to get teased and not get asked out on dates very often. At least I was sure that was the reason I had no dates, but it was probably my attitude more than my body size. I kept hoping to be really thin. After years of emotional suffering, I finally realized I did not have the bone structure to be thin, so I began to ask God to help me weigh what He wanted me to weigh.

I know that lots of young girls today are obsessed with being thin. Many of them even get drawn into eating disorders like bulimia or anorexia. These eating disorders will not solve their problem. The girls may lose weight, but they may also die and not be around to enjoy being thin.

God's Spirit is sent to you to be your Helper. You can feel free to talk to Him about anything you need help with, knowing that He will support you and give you aid.

Your Dating Relationships

There are many books to read and various teachings available on the rules of dating. Everyone has a formula, but I don't believe all of us can function under the same rules. Some teens are more mature at fifteen than some adults are at forty, and then some teens at eighteen still act as if they were ten. You should be led by your heart, and parents should be led by each teen's situation instead of setting hard and fast rules and trying to apply them to everyone.

I have two children who got married at age nineteen, and they both have very good, stable marriages. They always seemed to know in their heart that they would be married early. Neither of them had any great desire to date lots of different people; they just wanted to find the person God had for them and get married. Our other two children were in their early twenties when they got married, and they also have great marriages.

I don't feel I am qualified to say what age you <u>must</u> be to date, or to marry — obviously you should be mature enough before doing either, and only you, your parents and God know when that is. Some people say you should not even kiss someone unless you know it is the person you are going to marry. I don't feel that way, but the advice I would offer would be based on my opinion. Most people giving advice are giving their opinion, which is fine, but we must all be careful not to set forth our opinion as law.

However, I can say, and say very strongly, when it comes to dating and marriage, it is best to take it slow and easy. Don't be in a big hurry and end up getting in trouble. You have lots of time; the important thing right now is to grow up and enjoy life in the process.

Don't be pressured into having sex before marriage. Premarital sex may be popular with teens today, but it is not popular with God. Remember, if you follow His commandments, your life will be blessed. If you don't, you will reap what you sow.

The claim that "everybody is doing it" is not a reason for you to do it. If you have already been involved with someone sexually, that does not mean that God will not forgive you. You don't have to live under condemnation the rest of your life because you made a mistake, but you should take steps to discipline yourself in the future.

This is another area in which everyone needs boundaries. Draw a line beyond which you will not go, and don't keep moving it to suit the person you are dating. Don't put yourself in a position where you will be overcome with temptation. Do more double dating. Get more involved in group gatherings and activities. Avoid occasions when you are alone with your date without anyone else around. Do whatever you need to do to remain in a position where you can respect yourself and have the respect of others.

If someone asks you to live with them without being married to one another, "just say no." If the person doesn't think you are worth a full commitment, let God lead you to someone who does. Don't cheapen yourself by giving yourself away too freely. Don't allow someone to use you, then dump you when they are finished with you.

Don't try to replace the love you may not have gotten from your parents or others with a wrong relationship that will ultimately deepen your pain.

Above all, pray, pray, pray! That is the only way I know to avoid deception in relationships.

Our emotions can easily deceive us and make us think we are "in love," but we must know what love is — and it is certainly more than goose bumps, a pounding heart, heavy breathing and an excited feeling.

It is your right to own your emotions. By that I mean that you can have feelings and yet not permit them to rule you. You can really care about someone and yet have standards in your life that you refuse to compromise. If the other person truly cares about you, they will respect you for it.

There may be a lot of wickedness in our society today, but don't kid yourself — most people still know right from wrong. If you make right choices, others may act like they think you are "off the wall," but deep down inside they will respect you for it.

I believe most people in society are looking for someone who will stand up and make right choices — and you can be that "someone." You can be an example to your friends, not just another statistic of teenage pregnancy, drug addiction or alcoholism.

If you are confused about your feelings toward another individual, I recommend that you pray and be patient. God will reveal the truth to you in due time. Meanwhile, keep all of your relationships in the right priority, and they will be a tremendous blessing to you; otherwise, they can cause heartache and misery.

six

How to Handle Temptation

n order to stay out of trouble in life, we must understand the nature and dynamics of temptation. First of all, it will not go away; we all get tempted.

And when he was at the place, he said unto them, Pray that ye enter not into temptation.
Luke 22:40 KJV

For years I made the mistake of just wanting temptation to go away. I thought if I just would not get tempted to lose my temper, then I could stay peaceful all the time. Or if I did not have to endure the presence of people who aggravated me, then I could walk in love. It was a great day for me when I finally realized I was wanting something I would never have. I had to learn to face temptation, say no to it and gain the mastery over it.

You will have to do the same thing.

People are tempted in different areas depending on their specific individual weaknesses. I have always been more prone to get upset than my husband, so there were things that were a temptation for me that were not a temptation for him. I have never been tempted to rob a bank or a gas station, but there are people who are. Some are more tempted by food than others.

I recently heard someone say that we all have our own demons to face in life. That means we all have things that seem to be just too hard for us, but they won't be if we will learn to lean on God for the help we need.

In Luke 22:40 KJV quoted at the beginning of this chapter, we see Jesus telling His disciples to pray because they were about to be tempted. He was really telling them to pray for the strength they needed to avoid entering into the temptation that was coming, but He never told them to pray that it would not come.

In order to stand against the trials and temptations of this life, we must be strong — and we can be through our personal relationship with Jesus Christ.

Don't see yourself as a weak person who cannot resist temptation. Instead, believe that in Jesus you are more than a conqueror. (Romans 8:37.) Begin to see yourself strong against temptation.

The Lord's Prayer, with which most people are familiar, says, **And lead us not into temptation, but deliver us from evil. . . .**[1] God will deliver you from evil. He will give you the victory over it, if you pray and ask Him for help.

For example, if you need to lose weight and are tempted to overeat, pray for the strength to resist overeating before sitting down to the table or going through the drive-through at the fast-food restaurant.

Prayer is a privilege of your relationship with Jesus. You can ask God for anything in Jesus' name and be assured of receiving it, if what you are asking is in accordance with His will. (John 14:14.)

Avoid temptation as much as possible by staying away from the things that you know are tempting to you. The Bible says that we should avoid even the **appearance of evil.**[2] Separate yourself from people who try to tempt you to do things that go against your own conscience or that you know from God's Word to be wrong.

Living a righteous life brings a reward with it. If you make good choices, you won't be sorry. It may be hard for a period of time, but later on you will have the joy that everyone seeks.

My brother, who received the Lord a few years ago after many years in a lifestyle of alcohol, drugs and living with different women, said, "Living the Christian life is easy. What is hard is living a worldly life. You wake up sick with a hangover in the mornings, trying to figure out where to get money each day to buy drugs, and that is hard!"

Satan wants us to live for the moment and act as if tomorrow will never come, but it always does come, and we have to face the consequences of yesterday's decisions.

Use wisdom. Don't live on emotion alone. When the temptation in a specific area seems more than you can bear, think about this Scripture:

> **There hath no temptation taken
> you but such as is common to man:
> but God is faithful, who will not suffer
> you to be tempted above that ye are
> able; but will with the temptation**

**also make a way to escape, that ye
may be able to bear it.**

1 Corinthians 10:13 KJV

Everyone is tempted; it is a very common occurrence. But when Satan starts to put thoughts in your mind like "I can't stand this; I will have to give in," tell him he is a liar as the Bible says he is. Remember that God will show you the way out. Lean on Him and let Him help you.

Anytime you find yourself in trouble, cry out to God for help. You don't even have to speak out loud. Talk to God in your heart. If you are born again, He lives inside of you. Your heart has become His home, and He hears everything you say.

Those of us who endure temptation and don't give in to it will receive rewards from God. (James 1:12.) One of the rewards we will receive is the inner peace that comes from knowing we have done the right thing.

A guilty conscience is a hard pillow to try to sleep on. Making right choices is the only thing that can give peace, which leads to true joy.

It seems that today there has arisen an entire generation of people who are seeking peace. At least we hear a lot of talk about peace. But at the same time, many of the same people who say they want peace are making all the wrong decisions.

Violence, abortion, homosexuality, drugs, alcohol, premarital sex, popularity — none of these things will give you peace; they will, in fact, add to the pressure in your life.

Seek peace in the right place, which is in the will of God. That is the only place you will find it.

Jesus Understands

For we do not have a High Priest Who is unable to understand and sympathize and have a shared feeling with our weaknesses and infirmities and liability to the assaults of temptation, but One Who has been tempted in every respect as we are, yet without sinning.

Hebrews 4:15

The words "Jesus understands" bring great comfort to me. When nobody else understands us or what we are facing in life, Jesus understands. He understands temptation because He was tempted in every area in which we could possibly be tempted, and He successfully resisted each one of them.[3] He did it for us. He came to earth for us, not for Himself. He left His position in heavenly glory to come to earth in the form of a man to help us. He needed to experience what we experience in order to relate to us.

Yes, Jesus understands!

When you are tempted, you don't have to feel like some miserable, no-good failure. You can know that Jesus understands, and because He understands, you can run to Him for help in your time of temptation, as we are told in Hebrews 4:16:

> **Let us then fearlessly and confidently and boldly draw near to the throne of grace (the throne of God's unmerited favor to us sinners), that we may receive mercy [for our failures] and find grace to help in good**

time for every need [appropriate help and well-timed help, coming just when we need it].

One of the reasons we give in to temptation is that we are so hesitant to reach out for help.

You can share with the right friend what you are going through. Getting it out into the open will begin to reduce its power over you. Hidden things have more power than those exposed.

Satan wants us to keep things hidden; therefore, he tells us that nobody will understand but will judge us critically and reject us. We end up frequently keeping things to ourselves and fighting our battles alone, which is a mistake. Our strength is multiplied as we join forces with those around us who love us.

Don't isolate yourself. Open your heart to those who desire to help you.

You can run to Jesus. He understands. Go boldly to His throne in prayer, and let Him give you the help you need before it is too late. Don't keep making the same mistakes over and over in life — get the help you need!

seven

What Does Your Future Hold?

For I know the plans that I have for you," declares the LORD, "plans for welfare and not for calamity to give you a future and a hope."

Jeremiah 29:11 NASB

> *"For I know the plans that I have for you," declares the LORD, "plans for welfare. . . ."*
> *Jeremiah 29:11 NASB*

The question "What does the future hold?" is one to which we would all like clear-cut answers; however, God does not always give us a look at the future when we would like to have it.

Many teenagers feel pressured because people keep asking them about their future: "What are you going to do with your life? What kind of career are you going to pursue? Are you going to college? If so, which school have you chosen and what will your major be? If not, where are you going to work?" The questions seem to come continually, but many times teens don't know the answers themselves yet.

I have seen teens actually become very depressed because they don't have a clear-cut vision of their future. They sometimes become deceived into thinking they are the only ones who don't know what to do with their life.

If this describes you, you should realize that you are not the only one in that situation. Even the people you know who seem to have it all together may be in for some surprises.

When I started out in life, I thought I was going to be a bookkeeper. That was what I studied for and what I did on my first few jobs. Now I am a Bible teacher and television evangelist. I don't think I could have been any more wrong about what I thought my life's direction would be.

Actually, my direction was correct at the time, but like everything else, our course in life is progressive; finding God's will for us is progressive — we find it one day at a time, one step at a time.

I even took some wrong steps along the way to discover what the right ones would be.

If you don't know what you want to do, try some things and you will begin the process of elimination. You might try nursing and find you don't have the stomach for it, or you might try accounting and find it bores you. At least you will have eliminated two things you know you definitely don't want to do.

I am not advocating wildly trying all sorts of things without giving any serious thought to any of them, but I am presenting a positive way to move forward without fear of failure.

It is best to do something rather than to do nothing. People respect you for trying, not for sitting idle filled with confusion. If you don't know what you want to do for a career in life, then take some time to make your decision. Get a job of some sort so you can support yourself and wait for direction or desire. In the mean-time, enjoy yourself.

If you are eighteen years old and just out of high school, you don't need to worry about retirement just yet. You have some time to make up your mind about the future. Don't make your present miserable by worrying about your future.

Don't be pressured by other people who seem to demand answers from you that you don't have. Tell them that you don't know, and you can't tell them anything if you don't know anything. Also, don't feel stupid because you don't know. As I have already said, there are lots of people who don't know. It is much safer to admit you don't than to pretend you do just to impress people.

The important thing is that you do something, not that you know at the ripe old age of eighteen what all of life holds for you.

If you recall, I mentioned earlier that my son Dan did many different things in the ministry before he actually was released by God into the call on his life.

The same thing happened to the apostle Paul. He was called into the ministry and did different things for several years before God separated him and Barnabas for that to which He had specifically called them. (Acts 13:1-3.)

We all have a call on our life, something specific we are supposed to do, but we find out what it is as we go along. God knows the end from the beginning,[1] but we don't — we get to trust Him. If we do that, He will see to it that nothing in our life is wasted.

All the office experience I gained during my book-keeping years is a great benefit to me in helping me manage the large ministry we have today. I also spent some years in management in the business world. That time too has been very beneficial in helping me know how to manage hundreds of employees today.

Don't think you are wasting your life if you don't feel that you have really hit upon "The Thing" you want to do forever. Learn to "go with the flow," and that attitude will help you enjoy the journey.

Too many people are hurrying through life trying to get somewhere without even knowing where they are going. In the process, they never enjoy where they are right now.

I think it is a tragedy of the worst kind when we don't enjoy every day that God gives us. Until I learned to enjoy each day as it comes, I spent a lot of my life sad and confused. I hope and pray that my encouragement to you will prevent you from making some of the same mistakes I made.

Both of our daughters thought they wanted to work with the handicapped, so they obtained jobs at the Missouri School for the Blind. Each of them worked there about a year or less.

Actually, I don't think any of our children were thrilled at the thought of working for their parents in the ministry. The ministry part wasn't the problem; it was having Mom and Dad for a boss.

By the time children are grown, they want to have some distance and space to make their own decisions. I am sure our children thought they might lose that right if they worked for us.

We did not push any of them. We told them we would support their decision no matter what they chose to do. But we also told them we felt it was God's best for all of us to work together. Today they all work with us in the ministry along with their respective spouses. I am sure our grandchildren will also work for us someday.

The first time we offered our son-in-law Steve a job, he did not want to work with us. He thought it might create problems in the family if there were any issues on the job that needed confrontation. We just let it go. Shortly afterwards he was laid off and changed his mind about working with family. Today he realizes that it took that drastic change in his life for him to recognize what God's perfect will was for him and that he needed to get into it.

A similar thing happened to me after God called me into the ministry. I was working at a full-time job, and, I might add, it was a good one. I made good money, the company paid for my gasoline and there were other "perks" and benefits.

Then God began dealing with me about the call on my life and about preparing for it. I kept trying to do that but never seemed to have enough time. Finally, I went to a part-time job even though I knew in my heart that God wanted me to quit working entirely and trust Him and my husband to take care of me.

Since I was only doing part of what God was telling me to do, I was out of God's will. I got fired! I was accused of doing some things that I definitely did not do. Actually, the whole thing was ridiculous, but then things can easily get that way if we are not being totally obedient to God.

What am I trying to tell you through all this? Simply this: We are all prone to take the long route in getting to our destination in life. We do the best we know how, but our "know-how" is limited until we have lived long enough to get some experience.

When you feel as if you are wandering in life from one thing to another with no direction, don't be discouraged. It is not lost time because you are getting experience, and that is part of growing up.

Our children loved us but did not want to work for us. Now they all love their jobs and their parents. Admittedly we had to go through some difficulties to get from where we began to where we are now, but it was worth it.

Anything worth having is worth going through some discomfort to obtain.

Trade Reasoning for Trust

Trust in the LORD with all your heart, and lean not on your own understanding;

**In all your ways acknowledge Him,
and He shall direct your paths.**

Proverbs 3:5,6 NKJV

Proverbs 3 says we should trust God with all of our heart and mind and lean not on our own understanding, promising that He will direct our steps if we acknowledge Him. This means that we must stop trying to figure out things we can't figure out, worrying and being anxious about them. That includes our future. None of us has a guarantee about the future, so we must all learn to live one day at a time.

For many years, I was addicted to excessive reasoning, and that addiction was causing me to live a tormented life. Due to being abused in my childhood, I learned early in life that the best policy was to take care of myself and not ask anyone for anything.

I was always one step ahead of my life mentally, trying to plan out the next thing. In this way I felt I had control of what was going to happen to me. I thought that was the only way to prevent people from hurting me.

God had to work with me a long time before I finally learned that even though I was trying to figure out everything, I really was still not controlling my future. Often I thought I had things figured out and was sure they would happen a certain way, and then they did not occur that way at all. The only thing I had accomplished was wasting a lot of time with all my reasoning and figuring.

I finally realized that I had to trade worry and reasoning for trusting God if I ever wanted to be peaceful and enjoy my life. It took an entirely different approach to life, but I am very glad I made the transition.

Are you doing what I used to do? Are you so busy trying to figure out the future that in the process you are becoming more and more confused? If so, you are getting the same result from reasoning beyond the point of sensible planning that everyone else gets — confusion! If you will make a decision to trust God and wait on Him, He will give you discernment — He will give you spiritual understanding. Discernment comes to us in a supernatural way apart from what we know in the natural.

Sometimes we say, "I don't know what it is, but I just feel this is what I am supposed to do, or not supposed to do." What we feel right about in our hearts is usually more correct than what our thoughts tell us, unless the two agree. Be sure you feel peaceful inside about your decisions.

Discernment is what we also call intuition or revelation. We know something that we don't know the ordinary way, through learning and education.

We desperately need discernment in our life. It is one of the best ways to stay out of trouble and not waste time.

Discerning of spirits is one of the gifts of the Holy Spirit described by Paul in 1 Corinthians 12. Discerning of good and evil is another function of this spiritual gift. With it, not only can we tell who is motivated by good and who by evil, but we can discern what would be good for us and what would not. This gift is closely related to wisdom.

In our society today, everyone is seeking knowledge, but knowledge is of no real value without wisdom. Wisdom is the ability to properly apply knowledge. One definition of wisdom is "common sense."[2] We all do some things that really just don't make any sense.

Recently, I offered to take one of my daughters shopping and buy her some clothes. At first she did not know if she wanted to go out, but then she said, "I guess it wouldn't make much sense to turn down an offer like that." I responded that she was right; it wouldn't make any sense. So we went shopping. Her body did not want to get up and go, but her spirit helped her discern what the wisest action would be. At another time going shopping, even to get free clothing, might not be the best because you have another priority that is more important.

You can learn to live by wisdom in every area of your life. You don't have to live by just doing what everyone else thinks you should do. You can hear from God, be led by His Spirit and make quality decisions that will lead to a greater future.

The major thing that blocks discernment is using our own reasoning to try to get by logic answers God is trying to give us through discernment. Settle down, be patient and start trusting God to lead you into the future He has already planned and prepared for you. Don't worry or feel pressured if you don't know right this minute what you want to do with your entire life. Do something productive now, but be open to change.

As I mentioned previously, I was addicted to reasoning excessively. When we speak of addictions, we usually think only of drugs or alcohol, but there are mental and emotional addictions as well.

Some people, for instance, are addicted to approval. They need everyone's verbal approval to feel emotionally stable.

I had that problem as well as an addiction to reasoning. I could not feel comfortable and stop worrying until I felt I had the answer to everything. Often I thought I had the answer, but then God surprised me. When I finally learned to stop wasting my time trying to figure out things that God was not ready to show me, I was delivered from my addiction to reasoning.

I remember having withdrawal symptoms like a person might have when withdrawing from a substance addiction. The only difference was that my withdrawal symptoms were in the emotional realm instead of the physical realm.

I can remember how hard it was for me to refuse to think about all the things in the future to which I did not have answers. For example: "Where will we get the money to pay the repair bill on the car when it is due next month? What will we do if Dave gets laid off from his job? What will happen if I go in this certain direction with my life and it turns out wrong? What will people think of me? What will they say?"

The list goes on and on.

My mind was whirling with activity like this all day long and far into the night. I had such a habit of doing it that I was actually bored when I first began changing. I did not know what to do with my mind. I have since learned that I can think about things like how good God has been to me and what I can do to bless someone else. Actually, there are lots of great things to do with the mind that are productive; constantly reasoning to try to figure things out that we can't, however, is not one of them.

Learning to trust is also progressive. Like everything else, it requires stepping out a little bit at a time. This is especially frightening for those of us who have trusted others and been hurt repeatedly by them.

God is not like people, but having no experience with His faithfulness and goodness, we have nothing on which to base our faith except His Word. God's Word, of course, is enough, but initially we don't know that, so learning to trust God and His Word is not always quick or easy.

Don't be discouraged if these transitions I am speaking of take time. Also, don't be discouraged if they seem hard, or perhaps even almost impossible. Just don't give up. If you keep trying, you will make the changes necessary for a great life, trusting God being one of the major ones.

Previously, you may have felt that you had no answer to give people when they questioned you about the future. But now you have the best answer in the world. Just tell them, *I don't know what the future holds, but I do know the One Who holds the future. God has a good plan for my life, and He will reveal it to me — little by little.*

eight

Parents Are People Too!

Thus far in this book I have been speaking to teenagers, but in this final chapter I would like to talk to adults.

God created every teen (as well as every adult) to live a wonderful, successful, joy-filled life. But as we have seen, teens are under a great deal of pressure these days. Constant bombardment with negative feedback from adults adds to this pressure and often makes it difficult for teenagers to make right choices.

God has purposely placed our children in our life so that we can train them in the way they should go,[1] yet the teen years can be challenging for both age groups. While it is necessary for us as parents to set boundaries for them, it is also necessary for us to make a special effort to show them unconditional love and respect.

> *God has purposely placed our children in our life so that we can train them in the way they should go....*

You as parents can reach your teenagers with unconditional love, not judgment and criticism. We always love the person, but not necessarily their actions. Love can heal and change them.

Love for your teenager can be demonstrated in a variety of ways. For example, you can spend more time together as a family. This will enable you to develop healthy communication with them and show them how to draw upon God to meet their needs. Telling is not as effective as showing. Be a good example.

If you are already doing this kind of thing, don't stop. If you are not, I encourage you to start now. You may not see a change at first, but your persistence could be the very thing that keeps your teenager from becoming another teen statistic.

"What Is Wrong with These Kids Today?"

The following material is a list of statistics concerning teenage violence, suicide, pregnancy and substance abuse.

Usually when we adults read these types of statistics, our immediate thought is, *These teenagers today sure are causing a lot of trouble,* or, *What is wrong with these kids today?* I think it is time we look for the root of the problem and stop judging all young people by the fruit we see in the lives of some teenagers.

There is a reason for such widespread serious problems, and we will never get to the truth without being willing to look at ourselves also. Where have adults, the government and society in general failed? What is the real cause of statistics like these:

Teen Violence

The Centers for Disease Control and Prevention (CDC) reported that:[2]

- In 1997, 18.3 percent of high school students nation-wide carried a weapon (gun, knife or club) during the thirty days preceding the survey.

- 7.4 percent of high school students were threatened or injured with a weapon on school property in 1997 during the twelve months preceding the survey.

- Homicide is the second leading cause of death for persons 15-24 years of age.

- The rate of homicide among males ages 15-19 was 22.6 percent in 1997.

- 36.6 percent were in a physical fight during 1997.

- 6,146 young people ages 15-24 were victims of homicide in 1997. This amounts to an average of 17 youth homicide victims per day in the U.S.

- 85 percent of homicide victims ages 15-19 were killed with a firearm in 1997.

The Center for the Prevention of School Violence —
North Carolina Department of Juvenile Justice and
Delinquency Prevention says that:[3]

- Elementary school students are just as likely as those
  in secondary schools to be the victim [sic] of a violent
  act. (The Metropolitan Life Survey of the American
  Teacher, 1999: Violence in America's Public Schools —
  Five Years Later, Metropolitan Life, 1999)

- Peer group pressure is cited by 50 percent of seventh
  through twelfth graders as a major factor in why
  violence occurs in schools. Drugs or alcohol is cited by
  39 percent; lack of parental supervision is cited by 36
  percent; and lack of family involvement by 25 percent.
  (The Metropolitan Life Survey of the American Teacher,
  1999: Violence in America's Public Schools — Five
  Years Later, Metropolitan Life, 1999)

- The juvenile gang problem affects communities of all
  sizes and all regions in the U. S. with the number of
  gang members rising in small cities and rural counties
  in the late 1990s. (OJJDP Research: Making a
  Difference for Juveniles, Office of Juvenile Justice and
  Delinquency Prevention, 1999)

- The violent victimization rate for students in schools
  where gangs were reported was almost 8 percent
  compared to the 3 percent rate for students in
  schools with no reported gang presence. (Juvenile
  Offenders and Victims: 1999 National Report, Office of
  Juvenile Justice and Delinquency Prevention, 1999)

- Violent crimes by juveniles peak in the afternoon
  between 3 P.M. and 4 P.M., the hour at the end of the
  school day. (Juvenile Offenders and Victims: 1999
  National Report, Office of Juvenile Justice and
  Delinquency Prevention, 1999)

Teen Sex, Pregnancy and Abortion

According to a 1998 <u>USA Today</u> article on male teens' responsibility in teen pregnancies:[4]

- Teen-age boys begin having sex at an earlier age than girls do. They typically have more sexual partners. Although most boys have had sex by their 17th birthday, they use condoms inconsistently at best.

- About 1 million teen-age girls become pregnant every year. More than half of them have babies. This is a $6.9 billion public health problem.

- Percentage of teen-age boys who have had sex:

Age 15	Age 16	Age 17	Age 18	Age 19
27%	45%	59%	68%	85%

Number of partners in the past year:

- 0 partners   10%
- 1 partner   44%
- 2 partners   26%
- 3-4 partners   14%
- 5 or more partners   6%

Condom use in the past year:

- Inconsistent or no use: 56%
- Consistent use: 44%

Pregnancy and birth — all male teens:

- 14% fathered a child

The National Center for Chronic Disease Prevention and Health Promotion says that:[5]

- The United States has the highest teenage pregnancy rate of all developed countries.

- Out of about 1 million teenagers who become pregnant each year, 95 percent of those pregnancies are unintended and almost one third end in abortions.

According to an article about teens published in the May 2000 issue of Newsweek:[6]

- In 1997, 48 percent of high school students had had sexual intercourse.

Teen Drug and Alcohol Abuse

According to research on teen alcohol and drug usage done by the National Council on Alcohol and Drug Dependence (NCADD):[7]

- 80 percent of high school seniors have used alcohol, 50 percent have used marijuana and 10 percent have used cocaine (NBIDA, 1999 "Monitoring the Future Study, Secondary School Students").

- First use of alcohol typically begins around age 13; marijuana around age 14 (NIDA, "Drug Use Among Racial/Ethnic Minorities," 1995, p. 31).

- Among teenagers who binge drink, 39 percent say they drink alone, 58 percent drink when they are upset, 30 percent drink when they are bored and 37 percent drink to feel high (OIG, HHS, "Drinking Habits, etc.").

- Approximately 9 percent of the nation's eighth graders, 22 percent of tenth graders and 33 percent of twelfth graders have been drunk during the last month;

12 percent, 22 percent and 26 percent respectively, have used an illicit drug (NIDA, 1999 Monitoring the Future Study, Secondary Students).

- In 1995, 21.5 percent (262,112) of the clients admitted to alcohol or other drug treatment programs were under age 24, including 18,194 under age 15 (Substance Abuse and Mental Health Services Administration, National Admissions to Substance Abuse Treatment Services, Advance Report No. 12, 2/97, p. 30).

- Researchers estimate that alcohol use is implicated in one- to two-thirds of sexual assault and acquaintance or "date" rape cases among teens and college students (OIG, HHS, "Youth and Alcohol: Dangerous and Deadly Consequences," Washington, DC, 4/92).

- 80 percent of teenagers don't know that a 12 oz. can of beer has the same amount of alcohol as a shot of whiskey; similarly, 55 percent don't know that a 5 oz. glass of wine and a 12 oz. can of beer have the same amount of alcohol (OIG, HHS, "Drinking Habits, etc.").

- 30 percent of children in grades four through six report that they have received "a lot" of pressure from their classmates to drink beer, 31 percent to try marijuana and 34 percent to try cigarettes (The Weekly Reader National Survey on Drugs and Alcohol, Middletown, CT, Field Publications, Spring 1995).

- A survey of high school students found that 18 percent of females and 39 percent of males say it is acceptable for a boy to force sex if the girl is stoned or drunk (OIG, HHS, "Dangerous and Deadly Consequences").

- Teenagers whose parents talk to them regularly about the dangers of drugs are 42 percent less likely to use drugs than those whose parents don't, yet only 1 in 4 teens reports having these conversations (Partnership for a Drug-Free America news release, 4/26/99).

The National Institute on Drug Abuse's (NIDA) 25th annual Monitoring the Future (MTF) study shows that:[8]

- The percentage of 12th graders who had ever used the club-drug ecstasy increased from 5.8 in 1998 to 8.0 in 1999; the percentage who had used ecstasy in the past year increased from 3.6 in 1998 to 5.6 in 1999; the percentage of 12th graders using ecstasy at least once in the past month prior to being surveyed increased from 1.5 in 1998 to 2.5 in 1999.

- The percentage of 10th graders who had been drunk in the past year rose from 38.3 in 1998 to 40.9 in 1999.

- The percentage of 8th graders having five or more drinks during the two weeks prior to being surveyed increased from 13.7 in 1998 to 15.2 in 1999.

- Among the graduating class of 1999, 54.7 percent of students had used an illicit drug by the time they reached 12th grade.

- Use of any illicit drug in the past year by 12th graders increased from 41.4 percent in 1998 to 42.1 percent in 1999.

Lifetime Prevalence of Drug Abuse, 1999: Monitoring the Future Study

	8th-Graders	10th-Graders	12th-Graders
Marijuana	22.2%	40.9%	49.7%
Cocaine	4.7	7.7	9.8
Inhalants	19.7	17.0	15.4
LSD	4.1	8.5	12.2
Heroin	2.3	2.3	2.0
Alcohol	52.1	70.6	80.0

The 1998 National Household Survey on Drug Abuse conducted by the Substance Abuse and Mental Health Services Administration (SAMHSA) states that:[9]

- 9.9 percent of youths ages 12-17 reported current use of illicit drugs in 1998.

- 8.3 percent of youths ages 12-17 were current users of marijuana in 1998.

- An estimated 1.8 million (0.8 percent) Americans age 12 and older were current users of cocaine in 1998.

- An estimated 1.1 million youths ages 12-17 met diagnostic criteria for dependence on illicit drugs in 1997 and 1998.

- 56 percent of youths ages 12-17 reported marijuana was easy to obtain in 1998; 21 percent said it was easy to obtain heroin; 14 percent of youths reported being approached by someone selling drugs during the thirty days prior to the interview done in conducting this survey.

- 10.5 million current drinkers were ages 12-20 in 1998. Of this group, 5.1 million engaged in binge drinking, including 2.3 million who would also be classified as heavy drinkers.

Columbia University College of Physicians & Surgeons Complete Home Medical Guide says:[10]

In the United States, drug use by teenagers follows a clear-cut sequence.

1. Beer and wine are the initial drugs used by teens.

2. Tobacco and hard liquor are used after introduction to beer and wine.

3. Marijuana is tried, often together with alcohol.

4. Illicit drugs such as psychedelics or heroin may be used after or in conjunction with marijuana.

This sequence does not indicate that all teenagers inevitably experience all of these steps. Use of beer or marijuana does not always lead to use of other drugs such as psychedelics, heroin or cocaine.

Teenagers are primarily influenced by their parents and their peers through:

- Cigarette smoking: Almost exclusively determined by peer pressure, although parents who smoke increase the chances of children smoking.

- Hard liquor use: Drinking patterns are often learned from parents.

- Marijuana use: Usually initiated through friends and peers.

- Illicit drug use: Usually associated with poor relationships with parents, exposure to parents and peers who misuse drugs and by depression or psychological distress.

Teen Suicide

The Surgeon General's Call To Action To Prevent Suicide report states that:[11]

- Between 1952 and 1996, the reported rates of suicide among adolescents and young adults nearly tripled.

- From 1980 to 1996, the rate of suicide among persons ages 15-19 years increased by 14 percent and among persons ages 10-14 years by 100 percent.

- Among persons ages 15-19 years, firearms-related suicides accounted for 96 percent of the increase in the rate of suicide since 1980.

- For young people 15-24 years old, suicide is currently the third leading cause of death, exceeded only by unintentional injury and homicide.

- More teenagers and young adults die from suicide than from cancer, heart disease, AIDS, birth defects, stroke, pneumonia, influenza and chronic lung disease combined.

- Suicide is currently the fourth leading cause of death among children between the ages of 10 and 14 years.

According to an article about teens published in the May 8, 2000, issue of <u>Newsweek</u>:[12]

- Anxiety disorders are the most pervasive psychiatric problems in teens.

- 13 percent of children between 9 and 17 suffer conditions ranging from chronic worrying to severe social phobia. The big concern with this is suicide, which is highly associated with depression.

- The rate of suicide was three times higher among males in the 1990s than it was in the early 1960s.

- Every year, one in 13 high-school students attempts suicide.

- Girls try to kill themselves more often than boys, but boys succeed far more frequently.

Teen Eating Disorders

In an article about teens published in <u>Time</u> magazine in 1998:[13]

- 2 million Americans — most of them women and girls — suffer from eating disorders. In the most extreme cases they literally starve themselves to death. Those who survive are at greater risk of developing brittle bones, life-threatening infections, kidney damage and heart problems.

153

- Approximately 1 in 150 teenage girls in the U.S. falls prey to anorexia nervosa, which can be defined as the refusal to eat enough to maintain even a minimal body weight.

- Anorexia has been diagnosed in girls as young as 8 years old.

According to the May 8, 2000, <u>Newsweek</u> article about teens:[14]

- More than half of all teen girls say they are or should be on a diet. They incessantly battle the 40 pounds they naturally gain as they grow between the ages of 8 and 14.

- About 3 percent of girls take it to the extreme, spiraling into bulimia or anorexia.

- There are no precise numbers, but researchers say eating disorders appear to be on the rise, affecting children as young as 8 years old.

- While far more common in girls, boys are also vulnerable.

- Boys have their own obsession: the muscular look.

- Creatine, an amino acid supplement used by athletes to build muscle power, is the latest "hot new thing" among teen boys. Most assume that it is harmless, but its safety has not undergone long-term testing.

Close the "Gap"

Having read these statistics, are you beginning to realize that the problems among teenagers are concurrent with problems in our society such as the rising divorce rate in the world today, the increased level of stress, advertising that has no moral guidelines, greed, and movies and television programs that are filled with violence, profanity, nudity and humanism?

There is a saying in the computer industry, "Garbage in, garbage out." If we adults are feeding our young people garbage, how can we expect to get anything else out of them? We are supposed to be their teachers, leaders, heroes and examples.

I realize that some teenagers will get into trouble even if they have almost perfect parents and an excellent atmosphere in which to grow up. But I also realize that adults must take some responsibility and make some changes.

Remember, we are told in God's Word, **Train up a child in the way he should go: and when he is old, he will not depart from it.** It is not uncommon for children who have been taught right to go astray or, so to speak, "sow some wild oats" for a period of time. But usually children with a proper home life and consistent godly training from their leaders will not get into the kind of trouble represented by the statistics we have just seen.

As tragic as such facts are, notice one of those statistics states that parents who consistently talk with their teens about the problems with drugs experience a higher percentage of fewer negative incidences among their teens. It seems likely that parents who discuss the problems of alcohol and other wrong behavior with their teens will also experience similar results.

Am I saying that teens have no responsibility for their lives and that all their bad behavior is someone else's fault? No! Emphatically no! We must all eventually take responsibility for our own choices. I certainly lived in a less than desirable atmosphere while growing up, but I eventually took responsibility for my life and made changes that have led me into a fruitful, successful lifestyle.

I am saying that I am tired of watching adults act as though teenagers are not even people, especially the ones who seem to be rebellious or different from the so-called norm. The way many teens act is a cry for help. They are saying, "Somebody please notice me." They are crying out for love and acceptance, not judgment and rejection.

My hope is that this book will bring the teenage population and the adult population together in love and shared caring for and about one another. "The generation gap" is a commonly used term today. Why must there be a "gap" between us and our children? Can't we humble ourselves to learn about one another?

I have decided to learn more about teens, what their needs are, how I can help them, how I can be their friend and offer them acceptance and unconditional love. God is changing my heart and my attitude. I pray that you will ask Him to do the same for you.

I believe we will reap what we sow; it is a spiritual law and always works. If we sow mercy, we will reap mercy. If we sow judgment, we will reap what we have sown. Surely if we will begin to sow love, acceptance, understanding and a positive attitude, we will begin to reap the same from those whose lives we sow into.

Yes, <u>teenagers are people too</u>! They are not some other breed or species.

It took me until the year when I was working on this book to realize that my younger son will probably never show up at work in a three-piece suit with his hair parted on the side and neatly styled like his dad wears his.

I have decided that the baggy pants and new clothes that look worn out when purchased by today's teenagers are no worse than the style of casual clothes my generation wore when we were growing up in the 1950s. Before we adults judge our teens, we had better take a closer look at some of the things we did when we were their age.

Let's make a decision to breed respect in teens by showing them respect. Let's honor them. If we will do so, I believe they will honor us. Let's be for them, believe in them, give them opportunities to become an important part of our society.

Yes, we do have some serious problems today, but I know my God. If we will do our part, He will get involved and do His.

Our Kids Need God Today

The answer to "What is wrong with these kids today?" is: Our young people need God today. When prayer was allowed in our classrooms and the Ten Commandments were on the walls of our schools, children at least had something to direct them, even if they were not being properly directed at home.

Since prayer, in 1962, and the Ten Commandments, in 1980, were removed from schools, and people began to fall away from God, prayer and the teachings of the Bible, there has been a gradual lowering of moral standards until the problems in society have reached today's magnitude as seen in the statistics in this chapter.

According to the 1995 National Household Survey (NHS) on Drug Abuse, between 1964 and 1994 drug and alcohol abuse by American adolescents (ages 12–17) increased drastically.[15] First-time abusers of marijuana, cocaine, inhalants, hallucinogens and alcohol increased by 1,600 percent, 820 percent, 11,100 percent, 2,000 percent and 277 percent, respectively.

A 1996 article in U.S. News stated that homicide by youths under 17 tripled between 1984 and 1994.[16] The disregard for life and lack of other values very likely result from the years of no longer acknowledging God in the schools. The same article quotes the president of a national juvenile judges' group, Judge David Grossmann of Cincinnati, as saying, "Gangs have become the alternative to a nurturing family."[17]

We live in a society that was built on the foundation of God's Word. That foundation cannot be removed without creating a catastrophe. That is exactly what we have done.

We need God back in society, in every home, acting as the glue that holds marriages and families together. We need God in our lives today, and it has not been the teens who have removed Him. We must take responsibility for being passive and doing nothing while our homes and our society are being destroyed.

Legislature will not solve our problems. Neither will marching or demonstrating. Complaining certainly won't, nor will passivity or simply doing more of what we have been doing. We need a change!

We need to aggressively do whatever we can do for our teenagers, who will be the next generation to lead society. What can we do? As previously mentioned, we need to love them. And we need to give them hope. We need to let them know they have a wonderful future ahead of them if they will learn how to exercise their free will to make right choices.

We also need to pray.[18] As we do, God will move, we will see the restoration of what we have lost and begin to have peace, unity, love, joy, hope and all the other things we truly need in this life — especially in our relationship with our teenagers!

Conclusion: Your God-Given Right to Enjoy Life

I have written this book because I want you to know that the pressures of growing up don't have to drag you down and keep you from succeeding in life. In the midst of the problems most teenagers face today, it is still possible for you to have peace and joy in your life and in your relationship with your parents.

It has not been my intention to tell you what to do or what not to do, but to let you know that you have a God-given right to enjoy your life and to become all that you can possibly be in Christ.

We all have areas in our life that need improvement. If ignored, they can prevent us from reaching our full potential. With

> *. . . you have a God-given right to enjoy your life and to become all that you can possibly be in Christ.*

God's help and by applying the biblically based principles in this book, you will be on the road to improving those areas in your life and developing your potential to reach your destiny — one that includes coming together with adults in a loving, caring and respectful relationship.

I pray that this book has helped you, inspired you and encouraged you to get started walking in the good life God has for you. Read it again and pass it on to a friend. And please feel free to visit our web site, call or write my office if we can help you.

I believe that God has exciting things on the horizon for you, that your best days are ahead. As you press forward in Him, my prayer is that He will richly and radically bless your life and that you will be a blessing to many!

Endnotes

Preface: [1]Numbers 14:1-9. **Chapter 1:** [1]See Ephesians 1:3; John 15:13-15. [2]2 Corinthians 5:17. [3]Matthew 1:20-23. [4]1 Peter 1:19-21. [5]1 Corinthians 15:3-8. [6]See Psalm 18:1-17. [7]Hebrews 13:5 NKJV. [8]See Genesis 8:22; Galatians 6:7. [9]Isaiah 55:8,9. **Chapter 2:** [1]See Ephesians 3:20. [2]John 14:16-18. [3]Matthew 10:30. [4]Acts 10:34. **Chapter 3:** [1]The word fear is derived from the Greek word phobos, which, in its earliest form, meant "'flight,' that which is caused by being scared; then, 'that which may cause flight.'" W.E. Vine, Merrill F. Unger, William White Jr., Vine's Complete Expository Dictionary of Old and New Testament Words (Nashville: Thomas Nelson, Inc., 1984), "New Testament Section," pp. 229-230, s.v. **"FEAR,"** A. Nouns; [2]See Isaiah 14:12-20; "[Lucifer.] The Roman name for the morning star (Hebrew [helel], 'the bright one'), which speedily disappears before the far greater splendor of the sun. This title is addressed to the king of Babylon... as a representative or embodiment of Satan, who is regarded as the power behind the king's throne.... The ignominious downfall of the tyrant of Babylon, prophetically pictured here... reflects upon Satan, his lord." THE WYCLIFFE BIBLE COMMENTARY, edited by Charles E. Pfeiffer and Everett F. Harrison, Electronic Database. Copyright (©) 1962 by Moody Press. All Rights Reserved. See Luke 10:18. [3]See John 8:44, Revelation 12:9. [4]See Genesis 1:26,27; Genesis 2:18-23. [5]See Genesis 3:17-19. [6]See John 3:16; Philippians 2:6-8. [7]See John 10:10.

[8]Webster's II New World College Dictionary, (Boston/New York: Houghton Mifflin Company, 1995), s.v. "manipulator." **Chapter 4:** [1]See 1 John 5:4 KJV. [2]See Hebrews 8:12 KJV. [3]John 8:11 KJV. [4]Malachi 3:6 [5]See John 10:30 KJV; [6]1 Corinthians 10:4. [7]Numbers 23:19. [8]See 1 Thessalonians 2:13. [9]1 Samuel 16 and 17. **Chapter 5:** [1]Matthew 7:12. [2]1 Samuel 16:7, John 7:24, John 8:15. [3]God is the same as His Son Jesus, and John 15:14 says that we are His friends if we do the things that He commands us to do. [4]See 2 Corinthians 12:9. **Chapter 6:** [1]Matthew 6:13 KJV. [2]1 Thessalonians 5:22 KJV. [3]Hebrews 4:14,15. **Chapter 7:** [1]See Isaiah 46:9,10; [2]Webster's II, s.v. "wisdom." **Chapter 8:** [1]Proverbs 22:6 KJV. [2]Based on research from CDC's 1997 "Youth Risk Behavior Survey" (YRBS). YRBS is a school-based survey designed to produce a nationally representative sample of risk behaviors among students in grades 9-12. Some material is based on a report presented by CDC's National Center for Injury Prevention and Control (NCIPC) called "Youth Violence in the United States." CDC studies youth violence on an ongoing basis; available from http://www.cdc.gov/od/oc media/fact/violence.htm, http://www.cdc.gov/od/oc/ media/fact/youthrisk.htm, and http://www.cdc.gov/ncipc/ factsheets/yvfacts.htm. [3]Research based on the Center for the Prevention of School Violence findings from 1999. Findings provide information reflective of different perspectives, different grade levels and different problems; available from www.cpsv.org. [4]Based on research from the article "Boys have role, too, in curbing teen pregnancy," USA Today (January 6, 1998), Editorial page; available from Archives in http://www.usatoday.com. [5]Based on research

done by the CDC's National Center for Chronic Disease Prevention and Health Promotion regarding teen pregnancy; available from http://www.cdc.gov/nccdphp/tpartner.htm. [6]Based on research done by the CDC and mentioned in the article "The Naked Truth," <u>Newsweek</u> (May 8, 2000), p. 58. [7]Based on research done in December 1999 by the National Council on Alcohol and Drug Dependence, Inc. NCADD is a national voluntary health organization that provides education, information and help about alcoholism and other drug addictions; available from http://www.ncadd.org/index.html. [8]Based on NIDA's national survey that tracks drug use trends among America's adolescents in 8th, 10th and 12th grades. It is funded by NIDA and conducted by the University of Michigan's Institute for Social Research; available from http://www.drugabuse.gov/NIDAHome1.html. [9]Based on research from the 1998 "National Household Survey on Drug Abuse." The survey is conducted annually by SAMHSA and is based on a nationally representative sample of the U.S. population ages 12 years and older; available from http://www.samhsa.gov. [10]Based on research from <u>Columbia University College of Physicians & Surgeons Complete Home Medical Guide</u> — "**TEENAGERS AND DRUGS**"; available from cpmcnet.columbia.edu. Columbia University in the City of New York is affiliated with the Columbia-Presbyterian Medical Center. The medical center is a "key component" of the university. [11]In July 1999, Tipper Gore and Surgeon General David Satcher presented this document at a press conference as a suicide prevention blueprint, which can be used by individuals, communities, organizations and policymakers;

available from http://www.surgeongeneral.gov/library/call-toaction/default.htm. [12]Claudia Kalb, "Unhealthy Habits," Newsweek (May 8, 2000), p. 68. [13]Christine Gorman, "Disappearing Act," Time (November 2, 1998, Vol. 152, No. 18); available from Archives in http://www.time.com. [14]Newsweek, p. 66. [15]Robert L. Maginnis, "The Facts About Teen Drug Abuse: What the Surveys Say," Insight, Family Research Council. The article's facts are based on research from the National Household Survey (NHS) on Drug Abuse, 1995. "Marijuana First-Time Adolescent Abusers, 1964-1994, Figure 1," "Cocaine First-Time Adolescent Abusers, 1964-1994, Figure 2," "Inhalant First-Time Adolescent Abusers, 1964-1994, Figure 3" and "Hallucinogen First-Time Adolescent Abusers, 1964-1994, Figure 4." NHS is a representative national sample conducted annually since 1971. Since 1992 NHS has been supported and directed by the Substance Abuse and Mental Health Services Administration, part of the U.S. Department of Health and Human Services. Available from http://www.frc.org/insight/is96i1dr.html. [16]Ted Gest with Victoria Pope, "Crime Time Bomb," U.S. News (March 25, 1996). Available from http://www.usnews.com/usnews/issue/crime.htm. [17]Ibid, available from http://www.usnews.com/usnews/issue/crime.htm. [18]The Bible, God's Word, contains God's thoughts and ideas about things and is a powerful weapon against our enemy Satan. It is every believer's defense and victory. (See Ephesians 6:17.) One of the best ways to pray for your teenager is by praying God's Word and inserting your teen's name in the Scripture. For example, pray Isaiah 54:13 for your teen by saying, . . . **all your** [say "my" instead of "your"] . . . **children** [say the name of your child here] **shall be disciples [taught by the Lord and obedient to His will], and great shall be the peace and undisturbed composure of your** [say "my" instead of "your"] **children** [say the name of your child here]. Look up the following Scripture references and pray them over your child: Isaiah 54:13; Isaiah 44:2,3; Psalm 115:14; Psalm 10:14; Psalm 72:4; Proverbs 11:21; Psalm 112:1,2; Isaiah 40:1,11; Philippians 1:6; Isaiah 59:21; Isaiah 61:9; Psalm 40:2,3; Romans 8:37; 1 Corinthians 15:57; Isaiah 49:25; Ephesians 3:20; Micah 7:8; 2 Peter 2:9; Colossians 1:9,10; 1 Peter 2:25; Micah 3:8; Romans 9:17; Isaiah 38:17.

About the Author

Joyce Meyer has been teaching
the Word of God since 1976 and in
full-time ministry since 1980. Previously
the associate pastor at Life Christian
Church in St. Louis, Missouri, she developed, coordinated, and taught a weekly
meeting known as "Life In The Word."

After more than five years, the Lord
brought it to a conclusion, directing her to establish her own
ministry and call it *"Life In The Word, Inc."*

Now, her *Life In The Word* radio and television
broadcasts are seen and heard by millions across the United
States and throughout the world. Joyce's teaching tapes are
enjoyed internationally, and she travels extensively conducting *Life In The Word* conferences.

Joyce and her husband, Dave, the business administra-
tor at *Life In The Word,* have been married for over 35
years. They reside in St. Louis, Missouri, and are the parents
of four children. All four children are married and, along with
their spouses, work with Dave and Joyce in the ministry.

Believing the call on her life is to establish believers
in God's Word, Joyce says, "Jesus died to set the captives
free, and far too many Christians have little or no victory in
their daily lives." Finding herself in the same situation many
years ago and having found freedom to live in victory
through applying God's Word, Joyce goes equipped to set
captives free and to exchange ashes for beauty. She believes

that every person who walks in victory leads many others into victory. Her life is transparent, and her teachings are practical and can be applied in everyday life.

Joyce has taught on emotional healing and related subjects in meetings all over the country, helping multiplied thousands. She has recorded more than 225 different audio-cassette albums and over 100 videos. She has also authored 51 books to help the body of Christ on various topics.

Her "Emotional Healing Package" contains over 23 hours of teaching on the subject. Albums included in this package are: "Confidence"; "Beauty for Ashes" (includes Joyce's teaching notes); "Managing Your Emotions"; "Bitterness, Resentment, and Unforgiveness"; "Root of Rejection"; and a 90-minute Scripture/music tape titled "Healing the Brokenhearted."

Joyce's "Mind Package" features five different audio tape series on the subject of the mind. They include: "Mental Strongholds and Mindsets"; "Wilderness Mentality"; "The Mind of the Flesh"; "The Wandering, Wondering Mind"; and "Mind, Mouth, Moods, and Attitudes." The package also contains Joyce's powerful book, *Battlefield of the Mind*. On the subject of love she has three tape series titled "Love Is..."; "Love: The Ultimate Power"; and "Loving God, Loving Yourself, and Loving Others," and a book titled *Reduce Me to Love*.

Write to Joyce Meyer's office for a resource catalog and further information on how to obtain the tapes you need to bring total healing to your life.

To contact the author write:
Joyce Meyer Ministries
P. O. Box 655
Fenton, Missouri 63026
or call: (636) 349-0303

Internet Address: www.joycemeyer.org

Please include your testimony or help received from this book when you write. Your prayer requests are welcome.

To contact the author
in Canada, please write:
Joyce Meyer Ministries Canada, Inc.
Lambeth Box 1300
London, ON N6P 1T5
or call: (636) 349-0303

In Australia, please write:
Joyce Meyer Ministries-Australia
Locked Bag 77
Mansfield Delivery Centre
Queensland 4122
or call: 07 3349 1200

In England, please write:
Joyce Meyer Ministries
P. O. Box 1549
Windsor
SL4 1GT
or call: (0) 1753-831102

Books by Joyce Meyer

Healing the Brokenhearted

"Me and My Big Mouth!"

"Me and My Big Mouth!" Study Guide

Prepare to Prosper

Do It! Afraid

Expect a Move of God in Your Life . . . **Suddenly**

Enjoying Where You Are on the Way to Where You Are Going

The Most Important Decision You'll Ever Make

When, God, When?

Why, God, Why?

The Word, the Name, the Blood

Battlefield of the Mind

Battlefield of the Mind Study Guide

Tell Them I Love Them

Peace

The Root of Rejection

Beauty for Ashes

If Not for the Grace of God

NEW: If Not for the Grace of God Study Guide

By Dave Meyer

Nuggets of Life

Available from your local bookstore.